愿你出走半生
归来仍是少年

[美]朱迪·赛佛斯等 著

张白桦 译

成长卷（中英双语）

世界微型小说精选

中国国际广播出版社

·自 ○ 序·

　　微型小说，又名小小说，今天已经成长为一个独立的文体。作为小说"四大家族"之一，进入"蒲松龄文学奖"和"鲁迅文学奖"的视野，成为当代受众范围最广的纯文学样式。这一成就的取得，与当代外国微型小说的汉译有着直接的关系。对此，我在《当代外国微型小说汉译的翻译文学意义》的论文中有过详尽的阐述。具体说来，就是推动中国当代主流文学重归文学性，引进了一种新型的、活力四射的文学样式，重塑了当代主流诗学，提高了文学的地位，从而创造了民族文学史、国别文学史上的"神话"，具有翻译文学意义。

　　微型小说翻译对于我来说，好像"量身定制"一般。20 世纪80 年代初，微型小说在中国横空出世，这种简约而不简单的文体非常适合我的审美取向和性格特征，而翻译则可以调动起我全部的知识和双语语言积累。从 1987 年我发表的第一篇微型小说译作《他活着还是死了》，到 2004 年的《我是怎样把心丢了的》，这十七年间，我完成的微型小说翻译总计约 350 万字。

I

我的微型小说创作有三种：第一种是母语原创，如《白衣女郎》。第二种是汉译英，如在加拿大出版的《中国微型小说精选》（凌鼎年卷），这是中国第一部英译微型小说自选集，我曾参与翻译。第三种是英译汉，这一种类所占比重最大。代表作有《爱旅无涯》《仇家》《爱你至深》等。

对于原作的主题，我更喜欢以人性探索为立足点的人文视角来选择、诠释。妇女、儿童和草根阶层等弱势群体始终是我关注的焦点。从内容上大体可分为治愈系、成长系、幽默系三个板块。

我选择翻译文本力求多种多样，如《爱你至深》的散文式，《杰作的诞生》的反讽式，《爱情草》的夸张式，《心愿》的叙事式，《女人也需要妻子》的议论式，《末日审判》的幻想式，《爸爸妈妈，为什么》的提问式，《睡丑人》的童话式，《求职》的书信式，等等。

我翻译时的期待视野定位在青年身上，目的是做文化、文学的"媒"，因此更愿意贴近读者，特别是青年读者，觉得"大家好才是真的好"。在翻译策略上以归化为主，异化为辅；在翻译方法上以意译为主，直译为辅；在翻译方式上以全译为主，节译为辅；在翻译风格上以时代性为特色，笃信"一代人有一代人的翻译"之说。

所幸这样的取向还是与读者和社会的需求相契合的，因而产生了一定的社会效益。首译都会发表在国内的百强、十佳报刊，如《读者》《中外期刊文萃》《微型小说选刊》《小小说选刊》《青年参考》《文学故事报》等。常见的情况是，在这样的权威报刊发表后，随即就会呈现"凡有净水处，即有歌柳词"的景观，如《爱你至深》发表的二十年间就被转载60余次。

转载不仅限于报刊之间，数十种权威专辑和选本的纸质版也有收录，如《21世纪中国文学大系翻译文学》、《外国微型小说三百篇》、《世界微型小说经典》（8卷）、《世界微型小说名家名作百年经典》（10卷）；电子版图书如《小小说的盛宴书系：别人的女郎》《诺贝尔文学奖获奖作家微型小说精选》等；网上资源如读秀、百链期刊、龙源期刊网等。

此外，众所周知，翻译微型小说历来是中考、高考、四六级的语文和英语考试的听力、阅读理解、翻译、作文的模拟试题和真题材料。书中的《想要有个家》《盲》《医生为什么迟到》《林中遇险记》等皆被改编过；翻译微型小说还是影视短剧、喜剧、小品的改编材料。

当然，还有社会影响。第一，多次荣获国家级奖项。1998年《爱旅无涯》获《中国青年报·青年参考》最受读者喜爱的翻译文学作品，2010年当选小小说存档作家，2002年《英汉经典阅读系列》获上海外国语大学学术文化节科研成果奖，2002年当选当代微型小说百家，2002年《译作》当选全国第四次微型小说续写大赛竞赛原作。第二，受到知名评论家张锦贻、陈勇等关注和评论达10余次。第三，曾受邀参加中央电视台、内蒙古电视台及电台、中国作家网的人物专访。第四，个人传记入选美国与捷克出版的《华文微型小说微自传》《中国当代微型小说百家论续集》《世界微型小说百家传论》。

第五，因为翻译而收到来自世界各地、各行各业的读者来信、电话、邮件不计其数。

虽然近年我转向长篇小说的翻译，并以《老人与海》《房龙地理》《鹿出没》等再次获得读者的青睐，然而对于我来说，那些年，绞尽脑汁一字一句地写在稿纸上，满怀希冀地一封一封地把译稿投进邮筒，忐忑不安地在报亭、邮局一本一本地翻找自己的译作，欢天喜地买几本回家，进门就问女儿"Can you guess?"等她的固定答案"妈妈又发了！"都是我生命中一个一个的定格瞬间。微型小说翻译是我的"初心"，而唯有"初心"是不能辜负的。因此，我于2015年开办了以我的微型小说翻译为内容的自媒体——微型公众号"白桦译林"，收获了大量读者和转载，更由于与张娟平老师的美好相识，促成了这三本书的整体亮相。

谨以此书感谢多年来扶持过我的报刊编辑老师，以及多年来一直乐于阅读我的微型小说的读者和学生。

目 ○ 录

content

女人也需要妻子 / Why I Want a Wife • 1

你今天过得好不好 / How Did It Go Today • 8

驯丈夫 / Taming Husband • 15

迷情药 / The Chaser • 19

你这一生 / Testimonial • 28

我为什么当老师 / Why I Teach • 46

书与友谊 / Companionship of Books • 53

想要有个家 / Home on the Way • 56

母亲的苹果 / Mother's Apple • 60

魔法大衣 / The Magical Coat • 65

四季梨树 / Four Seasons of a Tree • 70

我们都是破罐子 / The Cracked Pot • 72

幸福的人 / The Happy Man • 76

幸福在哪里 / Lessons of the Foreign Land • 85

I

实话实说 / Like the Sun • 98

伤不起 / The Sampler • 107

淑女 / Heavy Cerebral Metal • 112

跳楼姑娘 / The Falling Girl • 121

听，蟋蟀的声音 / The Cricket • 130

想做真人的稻草人 / The Scarecrow Who Wanted to Be a Man • 134

牧羊人的女儿 / The Shepherd's Daughter • 141

动物学校 / The Animal School • 148

感情岛 / Island of Feelings • 152

七色彩虹的传说 / A Story of the Rainbow • 156

睡丑人 / Sleeping Ugly • 161

小青蛙 / The Tiny Frog • 173

唯我论者 / Solipsist • 177

死神教父 / Godfather Death • 181

末日审判 / The Last Judgment • 189

两个狙击手 / The Snipers • 199

仇家 / The Interlopers • 209

交易 / The Deal • 219

医生为什么迟到 / Why the Doctor Was Late • 229

随意日 / Dressed Down • 234

生活是不是说不好 / Isn't Life Funny • 237

我终于恍然大悟 / I've Learned • 239

女人也需要妻子

【美】朱迪·赛佛斯

按照对于人的分类，我属于人们所熟知的妻子那类。我是一个妻子，而且，绝非偶然的是，我还是一个合法的母亲。

不久以前，我的一个男性朋友从中西部来了。他刚刚离了婚，唯一的孩子理所当然地由他的前妻抚养。很显然，他又在寻觅第二任妻子。一天晚上，我在熨衣服的时候想起他的种种，忽然萌生了一个念头：我也想要一个妻子。身为女人的我为什么也需要一个妻子呢？

我想重返校园学习，以便在经济上自立，支付自己的经济开支，如果需要的话，再供养那些依靠我的人。我要妻子边工作边供我上学。在我就读期间，我要求妻子照管孩子，并安排好医生给我和孩子们看病的时间。我要求妻子保证孩子们的饮食合理，保持孩子们的清洁卫生。我要求妻子为孩子们洗衣服、缝衣服。我要求妻子照顾孩子们的时候像一个训练有素的保育员，既要安排好他们的学业，又要保证他们与同伴之间有适当的社交生活，还要带他们去公园和动物园等地方。假如孩子生病了，我要求妻子去照料。假如孩子需要特殊护理，她要去陪床，因为，我理所当然是不能够耽误课的。与此同时，我的妻子必须把工作安排好：既能舍弃一些上班时间，又不至于丢了饭碗。有时这意味着她的收入会减少一些，但我想我能容忍。毫无疑问，只要我妻子还有工作，她就应该安排和承担孩子们的一切生活费用。

我希望妻子满足我的生活需要。她要保证家里的一切都整洁有序，要随时跟在我和孩子们后面打扫才是。我要求妻子保证我的每件衣服都能随洗、随熨、随补，因需要及时更换。她还应该负责把我的个人用品放在合适的地方，让我在需要的时候可以信手拈来。我想要一个不仅会做饭，而且还要做得一手好饭的妻子。我要求她制订食谱，作必要的采购，做好饭菜，笑吟吟地伺候我们就餐。然后我去看书学习，她把餐具清洗干净。我要求妻子在我偶染小恙时照顾我，对我生病、缺课深感同情。全家外出度假时，我要求妻子同行，以便在我们需要休息和换个环境的时候继续尽为人妻为人母的责任。

我需要这样的妻子：她不会像个家庭妇女似的对日常琐事絮絮叨叨让我烦心。当我就学习中遇到的某个难点大发议论时，我希望她洗耳恭听。在我完成论文写作以后，她会为我把论文打印出来。

我需要一个留意我社交生活中的每一细节的妻子。当我应邀会友的时候，我希望妻子做好孩子们的临时托管事宜。当我在学校结识了喜欢的人，想款待一番的时候，我希望妻子打扫房舍，烹制独具特色的菜肴，以供我和朋友们享用。在我和朋友们就某个共同感兴趣的话题高谈阔论的时候，她不会过来打断我们的谈话。我希望妻子在客人光临之前就妥善安置好孩子，让他们吃饱喝足，只差上床就寝，以免扫了我们的雅兴。我希望妻子细致入微地体察每一位客人的需求，使他们感到宾至如归：即确保有烟灰缸，将餐前小吃递给每一个人，主动询问是否需要添加食物，必要时随时斟满酒杯，给喜欢咖啡的人端上咖啡。我希望妻子理解我有时需要彻夜不归。

假如，我碰巧遇到了另一个女人，而她比我的现任妻子更适合做妻子的话，我希望我能有更换的自由。自然，我需要全新的生活。我的妻子要把孩子们带走，独自承担起抚养的全部责任，这样，我就可以自由自在，无拘无束了。

当我毕业找到工作以后，我希望妻子辞职回家，以便更完全彻底地尽为人妻的天职。

我的天，谁不想有个妻子？

Why I Want a Wife

By Judy Syfers

I belong to that classification of people known as wives. I am A Wife. And, not altogether incidentally I am a mother.

Not too long ago a male friend of mine appeared on the scene from the Midwest fresh from a recent divorce. He had one child who is, of course, with his ex-wife. He is obviously looking for another wife. As I thought about him while I was ironing one evening, it suddenly occurred to me that I, too, would like to have a wife. Why do I want a wife.

I would like to go back to school so that I can become economically independent, to support myself, and, if need be, to support those dependent upon me. I want a wife who will work and send me to school. And while I am going to school, I want a wife to take care of my children. I want a wife to keep track of the children's doctor and dentist appointments. And to keep track of mine, too. I want a wife to make sure my children eat properly and are kept clean. I want a wife who will wash the children's clothes and keep them mended. I want a wife who is a good nurturant attendant to my children, arranges for their schooling, makes sure that they have an adequate social life with their peers, takes them to the park, the zoo, etc. I want a wife who takes care of the children when they are sick, a wife who arranges to be around when the children need special care, because, of course, I cannot miss classes at school. My wife must arranges to lose time at work and not lose the job. It may mean a small cut in my wife's income from time to time, but I guess I can tolerate that. Needless to say, my wife will arrange and pay for the care of the children while my wife is working.

I want a wife who will take care of my physical needs. I want a wife who will keep my house clean. A wife who will pick up after my children, a wife who will pick up after me. I want a wife who will keep my clothes clean, ironed, mended, replaced when need be, and who will see to it that my personal things are kept in their proper place so that I can find what I need the minute I need it. I want a wife who cooks the meals, a wife who is a good cook. I want a wife who will plan the menus, do the necessary grocery shopping, prepare the meals, serve them pleasantly, and then do the cleaning up while I do my studying. I want a wife who will care for me when I am sick and sympathize with my pain and loss of time from school. I want a wife to go along when our family takes a vocation so that someone can continue to care for me and my children when need a rest and a change of scene.

I want a wife who will not bother me with rambling complaints about a wife's duties. But I want a wife who will listen to me when I feel the need to explain a rather difficult point I have come across in my course of studies. And I want a wife who will type my papers for me when I have written them.

I want a wife who will take care of the details of my social life. When my wife and I are invited out by my friends, I want a wife who will take care of the babysitting arrangements. When I meet people at school that I like and want to entertain, I want a wife who will have the house clean, will prepare a special meal, serve it to me and my friends, and not interrupt when I talk about the things that interest me and my friends. I want a wife who will have arranged that the children are fed and ready for bed before my guests arrive so that the children do not bother us. I want a wife who takes care of the needs of my guests so that they feel comfortable, who makes sure that they have an ashtray, that they are passed the hors d'oeuvres, that they are offered a second helping of the food, that their wine glasses are replenished when necessary, that their coffee is served to them as they like it. And I want a wife who knows that sometimes I need a night out by myself.

If by chance, I find another person more suitable as a wife than the wife I already have, I want the liberty to replace my present wife with another one. Naturally, I will expect a fresh, new life, my wife will take the children and be solely responsible for them so that I am left free.

When I am through with school and have acquired a job, I want my wife to quit working and remain at home so that my wife can more fully and completely take care of a wife's duties.

My God, who wouldn't want a wife?

你今天过得好不好

【加拿大】梅里尔·布朗·托宾

我已经做了两个星期的半日工，觉得这份工作很合自己的兴趣，薪水也不薄。

可是今天早晨，我却要哄不想上学的大儿子下车。"我今天不舒服，我想回家。"他哭闹着。我很清楚，他不过是有点咳嗽罢了，于是劝导他说，"你知道我上午得上班去，你要是病了的话，你的老师会通知我的，这样，我中午就可以把你带回家。"

最后，儿子伤心地走了，看到他眼泪汪汪的样子，我交叉着双手，担心我走了以后，他会不会哭。

中午，我把二儿子吉米从托儿所接回家，丁零零！丁零零！一进门就听见电话铃声，原来是女友。我们谈起了六个月以后的假期，二儿子早已不耐烦，嚷着要跟电话里的阿姨说话，还说饿了。我只好挂了电话。

砰！砰！有人敲门。

"你好，请进。"来的人是我的邻居，她每周有两个下午帮我照看小儿子，跟她的儿子一起玩。

"不进去啦，我得赶快回去，不过我得预先告诉你，我明天下午要参加一个葬礼，所以不能照看吉米了。"

就在我们互相安慰的时候，啪，啪，是雨点落下的声音。早晨我把前一天夜里洗出来的一大堆衣服晾出去了，"我的衣服！"我叫着，匆匆忙忙地跟邻居道了别。

等我跟跟跄跄地把衣服抱回来，吉米跑过来说："有电话。"

"喂。"

"喂，我是布伦达，你大儿子在单位呢，他说你中午要接他，我们给学校打电话询问，老师说不知道这回事，我们找你半天了。"

我去接大儿子之前在门上留了个条子，告知邮递员把邮包放在隔壁邻居家，就在这时，邮车到了，让人欣慰的是这件事还算正常，尽管这让我迟到的时间更长了，我还是挤出了一个笑脸。

到了单位，我看到大儿子欢蹦乱跳，笑嘻嘻的样子。病了？绝对不可能！我忙着向老板道歉、致谢，又浪费了不少宝贵时间。

接着，我又赶到学校跟校长和老师做解释："我现在可以把他送回学校来，只是他挨了我的一顿'剋'，这会儿还垂头丧气，所以，我想不如下午带他去医院做个检查，反正我与大夫事先恰好有个约会。"

嘟，嘟，嘟，我发动汽车时，啪的一声，车胎爆了。多亏我有先见之明，加入了一个汽车服务俱乐部，于是，我先给俱乐部打电话请修理工，然后又给医生打电话说明情况，对方说迟到半个小时没关系。

我边洗衣服边等修理工，二十分钟过后，他来了，修了一阵，说没问题。他走后，我把两个孩子抱上车，就按他所说的发动车，谁料车没发动，却往后跳了跳，我顿时觉得手脚冰冷，这到底是怎么回事？当然是离合器！离合器！

原来，我忘了踩离合器了。我踩了离合器，按照他的指令操作，车子终于优雅地启动了，我扫了一眼表，已经是差十五分三点了，太可怕了，女儿在三点半以后随时都有可能到家，现在找邻居帮着照看已经来不及了，但愿在医院不要耽搁太久。

在医院候诊室等候的那二十分钟期间，我四岁的小儿子把我好端端的衣服裤子都弄脏了。从托儿所回来以后，我已经给他洗过三次手了，可是现在还是那么脏，我都不好意思看。"叭！叭！黑绵羊！"他说了十遍。

最后，终于轮到我们了。

我把两个孩子推到前面，说我把这次约定的看病机会让给他。"一点儿细菌感染。"医生开了处方。想到下星期我会更忙乱，我壮着胆子请求医生给我们俩也看一看，他允了。

我们终于回了家，女儿还没回来，我松了一口气。

女儿回来以后，我赶忙开车出去买东西，心里想着丈夫会在去中学之前，在五点的时候回来喝茶，因为时间的关系，我只买了几样最基本的食品。

咝，咝，茶快熬好了。

"唔，你今天看起来真漂亮。"我丈夫说道，他回家以后打量着我还没来得及换下来的新外套。我急急忙忙跑来跑去，把还没有完全解冻的熟排骨做熟，还要注意不要弄脏了衣服。

他设法在我跑来跑去的时候吻了我一下，然后漫不经心地问我："你今天过得好不好？"

How Did It Go Today

By Meryl Brown Tobin

I had been working for a fortnight half-time and I had found the interest and the salary most rewarding.

But there I was this morning trying to kid my eldest, a reluctant eight-year-old to get out of the car at his school. "But I want to go home. I don't feel well," he blubbered. Knowing full well that he was not really ill and that except for a bit of a cough I told him, "You know I have to go to work till lunchtime today. Your teacher knows where I am and where to ring if you're sick. She can tell me and you can come over and I'll take you home at lunchtime."

Unhappy at the thought of leaving a distressed child, I crossed my fingers wondering that once I had gone he would get over his attack of the weeps.

I headed for home at midday in time to meet my second son as he came home from kindergarten. Ring, ring! The phone rang as I opened the door. It was one of my friends. We chat about the break six-month later. An impatient and hungry little boy ordered lunch so he had a chat with Auntie. Eventually I hang up.

Knock, knock, thudded the doorknocker.

"Hi, come in," I greeted the neighbor who minded my little chap, as company for her own son, two afternoons a week.

"No, thanks, I have to get back. But I thought I'd better let you know I won't be able to have Jimmy tomorrow. I have to go to a funeral."

While we commiserated together, splot, splot! Down came spots of rain. "My washing!" I cried, bidding my neighbor a quick good-bye. That morning I had managed to peg out one-load of washing which I had done the night before.

As I staggered in with the washing, Jimmy came running. "Mummy, there's someone on the phone," he said.

"Hello."

"Hello. It's Brende. We have your son here at work. He says you told him to meet you here at lunchtime. We've rung his school but they don't know anything about it. We've been trying to get on to you for some time."

Before I headed off to collect my elder son I went to re-stick a notice on the door telling an expected delivery man to leave my parcel next door. Simultaneously a delivery truck pulled up. Relieved that at least something had gone right even though it made me later than ever, I managed a smile.

At my place of work, an energetic, beaming boy ran out to

greet me. Sick? Not on your life! More precious time was lost while I apologized to and thanked my bosses for their trouble.

Then off to the school next door I went where I explained the situation to the principal and my son's teacher. "I'd make him come back to school now, but he's made himself so upset with my 'barking' at him that I'll take him with me. I have a doctor's appointment for myself so I might have him checked over at the same time."

Brrr, phtt. Brrr, phtt went the car as I tried to start it. Fortunately, with foresight, we had joined a car service club for my benefit. So I called for a mechanic to come out. Next I dialed the doctor's receptionist. She assured me it would not matter if I were up to half an hour late.

Going on with more washing which had to be done, I was interrupted twenty minutes later by the service man. Then off he went and I piled the two boys in the car once again. After carefully following the serviceman's instruction I was appalled when the car, instead of purring into life, jumped backwards. It did this two or three times and I turned cold. What was wrong? Of course, the clutch!

I applied the clutch and then followed his directions. The car glided gracefully back out of the drive. A glance at my watch showed it to be a quarter to three. Horrors, my daughter would return from school any time from three-thirty on. But it was too late to alert my neighbor to watch for her. I would just have to hope I was not help up at the doctor's.

During the twenty minute or so wait, my four-year-old scrambled all over my good pants suit. His hands, which I had expressly asked him to wash on three occasions since his return from kindergarten, were so grubby I was ashamed to look at them. "Baa Baa, Black Sheep!" he chanted it 10 times.

At last we were called.

Ushering in the two children before me, I explained to the doctor that I had given my appointment to my son, "A bit of a virus and a few wheezes," was his diagnosis. A quick script for an antibiotic made me bold enough to ask if he could squeeze the two of us in on the one appointment.

We finally headed home. I was relieved to find we had beaten my daughter there.

When she arrived it was back into the car so I could shop. Keeping in mind that my husband would soon be home for a five o'clock tea before he went off to high school, I was only able to shop for the bare essentials.

Sizzle, sizzle, the tea finally started to cook.

"Mm, you look nice," commented my husband, sizing me up in my new outfit when he came home. I was busily running round trying to cook only partly defrosted chops in a hurry and trying to avoid dirtying my clothes which I was too pressed for time to change.

He managed to kiss me on the run ant asked conversationally, "How did it go today?"

驯丈夫

【美】罗伯特·马克·奥尔特

　　从前，有个女人为自己的丈夫大伤脑筋，因为他不再爱她了：他对她熟视无睹，对她的喜怒哀乐也不太关切。

　　于是，女人向当地的一个巫师求助。她满含哀怨地向巫师倾诉了自己的凄惨境况，然后急切地问："你能施展魔法让他爱我如初吗？"

　　巫师沉吟片刻，答道："我可以助你一臂之力，不过，先决条件就是你必须给我搞到三根活狮子头上的毛，这是我为你施魔法所必需的。"

　　女人谢过巫师就离开了，快到家时，她在一块大石头上坐了下来，心中暗想：我怎么才能搞到三根活狮子头上的毛呢？的确，有只狮子常到村边来，可是，它样子凶猛，吼声骇人呢！她想啊想，最后终于想出了个办法。

　　于是，第二天一大早，她就抱了一只小羊羔来到那只狮子经常出没的地方，心急火燎地等啊等。最后，狮子终于出现了，渐渐走近。她迅速站起身来，把小羊放到狮子的必经之路上，就转身离开了。从那一天开始，她每天早晨都会早早地给那只狮子送一只羊羔。而狮子也渐渐地对这个女人熟识起来，她可真是个善解人意、体贴入微的女人。

　　没过多久，狮子只要一看见女人就会凑过来，让她抚摸自己的头和背。就这样，女人每天都会安详地、温情脉脉地抚摸狮子。直到有一天，她确信狮子对她已经完全信任了，才小心翼翼地从狮子的头上拔了三根毛，然后兴冲冲地向巫师的住所奔去。

"看呐，拿来啦，给你！"她一进门就兴高采烈地喊道，边喊边得意洋洋地递上了三根狮毛。

"你怎么这么聪明？你是怎么搞到的？"巫师吃惊地问道。于是，女人一五一十地叙述了全过程。

巫师听得很仔细，开始微微地笑着，继而笑容满面："去吧，用你驯狮的方法同样可以驯服你的丈夫。"

Taming Husband

By Robert Mark Ault

Once there was a woman who was greatly troubled by her husband. He no longer loved her. He neglected her and seemed to care little whether she was happy or sad.

So the woman took her trouble to the local magician. She told him her story, full of pity for herself and her sad condition. "Can you give me a charm to make him love me again?" she asked anxiously.

The magician thought for a moment and replied, "I will help you, but first you must bring to me three hairs from a living lion. These I must have before I can make the charm for you."

The woman thanked the magician and went away. When she came near to her home she sat down on a rock and began to think,

"How shall I do this thing? There is a lion who comes often near to my village, it is true. But he is fierce and roars fearfully." Then she thought again and at last she knew what she would do.

And so, rising early next morning she took young lamb and went to the place where the lion was accustomed to stroll about. She waited anxiously. At last she saw the lion approaching. Now was the time. Quickly she rose and, leaving the lamb in the path of the lion, she went home. And so it was that every day early in the early morning the woman would arise and take a young lamb to the lion. Soon the lion came to know the woman, for she was always in the same place at the same time every day with a young and tender lamb, which she brought for his pleasure. She was indeed a kind and attentive woman.

It was not long before the lion began to wag his tail. Each time he saw her and came close to her, he would let her stroke his head and soothe his back. And each day the woman would stay quietly stroking the lion, gently and lovingly. Then one day when she knew that the lion trusted her, she carefully pulled three hairs form him and happily set out for the magician's house.

"See," she said triumphantly as she entered, "here they are!" And she gave him the three hairs from the lion.

"How is it you have been so clever?" asked the magician in surprise.

And so the woman told him the story of how she had taken the hairs.

A smile spread over the face of the magician and, he said, "In the same way that you have tamed the lion, so may you tame your husband."

迷情药

【瑞士】约翰·格里耶

阿兰·奥斯汀紧张得像一只小猫一样，爬上了佩尔街一个黑洞洞的嘎吱作响的楼梯。他在灯光昏暗的平台上环顾良久，才在一扇门上认出了要找的那个字迹模糊的名字。

他按照事先被告知的那样推门长驱直入，发现自己站在一个小小的房间里，屋里没有什么家具，只有一张普普通通的餐桌，一把摇椅，一把平平常常的靠背椅，两个架子靠在一面烟熏火燎的脏脏的墙上，架子上摆着瓶瓶罐罐，大约有十几个。

一个老者坐在摇椅上看报纸。阿兰默默地递上别人给他的名片，老者非常客气地说："请坐，奥斯汀先生，很高兴认识你。"

阿兰问道："你有一种药……呃……有奇效，此话当真？"

老者回答："我亲爱的先生，我认为我卖的任何一种药——确切地说，都不可以用普通来描绘。"

"嗯，其实……"阿兰开了口。

老者打断了他的话头，从架子上取下一个瓶子，说："举个例子说吧，这是一种无色，并且几乎无味的水一样的液体，放进咖啡、酒和其他饮料中都不会被发现，就是尸体解剖也看不出来。"

"你的意思是毒药了？"阿兰惊呼，心中大惧。

"如果你愿意的话，称其为'生活清洁剂'吧，生活有时需要清洗。"老人漫不经心地说道。

"我不需要这样的东西。"阿兰说道。

"如此甚好，你知道要的什么价吗？一羹匙就够，我开价五千美元，绝不能少于这个数，一分都不能少。"老人说道。

"但愿你别的药没有这么贵。"阿兰忧心忡忡起来。

"哦，亲爱的，没这么贵，譬如迷情药就不会索要这么高的价，需要爱情的年轻人里面很少有人出得起五千美元，否则他们也不会需要迷情药了。"老者安慰阿兰。

"好呀，听你这么说，我很高兴。"阿兰说。

老者又说："我是这么看的，顾客如果对一种商品满意，需要另一种商品的时候，他就会回来，如果有必要，即便贵些，他也会攒钱来买。"

"这么说，"阿兰说，"你真的有迷情药卖了？"

"当然，可是只有心诚才灵哦。"老者边说边拿起另一个瓶子。

"可是这种药，不只……只……只……呃……"阿兰说道。

"哦，不对，其药效的应用范围并不限于唤起性冲动，换句话说，唤起性冲动只是它的一种功效，保证药效充分、强劲、有效、持久。"老者言之凿凿。

"哎呀！"阿兰惊叹不已。"太有意思啦！"

"不过，还要顾及精神层面。"老者又说。

"我的确已经想到了。"阿兰回答。

"迷情药用忠心耿耿代替漫不经心，以深情款款取代傲慢轻视，只要让女士服用一点点，那味道在橙汁、汤或者鸡尾酒里都不易察觉，不论她原来多么放浪轻浮，都会彻底改变，一无所求，只需要你，只想与你单独在一起。"老者解释道。

"我简直无法想象她会这样，她那么喜欢聚会。"阿兰说。

老者答道："她再也不会喜欢聚会了，因为怕你在聚会上结识漂亮姑娘，她会诚惶诚恐。"

"她会妒忌吗？她会吃我的醋吗？"阿兰欣喜若狂地叫着。

"正是，她会要求成为你的全部，要你终生依恋她。"

"她已经是我的全部了，我已经很依恋她了，只是她不在意。"

"她会在意的，只要她喝了这种药，她会非常地在意，你会成为她生命中唯一的兴趣。"

"太棒了！"阿兰喊了起来。

"她会要求对你的一举一动有知情权：你每天干什么，你说过的每个词，你想的每一件事，你忽然莞尔的原因，你面露悲戚的缘由。"老者说道。

"这才是爱情啊！"阿兰感叹。

"是啊，她会那么体贴入微地照顾你！绝不会让你累，让你坐在穿堂风里，不吃东西。你晚回来一个小时，她都会吓得六神无主，以为你被杀了，要不然就是被迷人的女人勾走了。"老者说。

"我简直无法想象戴安娜会变成这样！"阿兰叫道，喜出望外。

老者说："你不需要运用自己的想象力。顺便说一句，人总有被引诱的时候，假如你偶然失足，别担心，她最终会原谅你，即使她会深深受伤，但她最终会原谅你。"

"不会发生这种事情。"阿兰慷慨激昂地回答。

老者说道："希望不会，但万一发生了，你不必担心，她永远也不会跟你离婚，哦，不！而且，她自然也不会让你有一丝一毫的不自在。"

"那么，这种神奇的药多少钱？"

老者回答："不贵，不像我有时说的'生活清洁剂'那么贵，不贵。比你老的人才会依赖'生活清洁剂'，而且还得攒钱才能买得起。"

"那迷情药呢？"阿兰问。

"哦，这种药嘛，"老者边说边拉开餐桌的抽屉，取出一个小药瓶，"只要一美元。"

阿兰看着老者把药瓶装满，说道："我不知道怎么表达对你的感激。"

老者说："我乐于效劳。顾客用好了以后就会生出新的愿望，就会买更贵的药。给你药，你会感觉很有效。"

阿兰说："再次感谢，再见。"

"会再见的。"老者胸有成竹。

The Chaser

By John Collier

Alan Austen, as nervous as a kitten, went up certain dark and creaky stairs in the neighborhood of Pell Street, and peered about for a long time on the dim landing before he found the name he wanted written obscurely on one of the doors.

He pushed open this door, as he had been told to do, and found himself in a tiny room, which contained no furniture but a plain kitchen table, a rocking-chair, and an ordinary chair. On one of the dirty buff-colored walls were a couple of shelves, containing in all perhaps a dozen-bottles and jars.

An old man sat in the rocking-chair, reading a newspaper. Alan, without a word, handed him the card he had been given. "Sit down, Mr. Austen," said the old man very politely, "I am glad to make your acquaintance."

"Is it true," asked Alan, "that you have a certain mixture that has—er—quite extraordinary effects?"

"My dear sir," replied the old man, "I think nothing I sell has effects which could be precisely described as ordinary."

"Well, the fact is..." began Alan.

"Here, for example," interrupted the old man, reaching for a bottle from the shelf. "Here is a liquid as colorless as water, almost tasteless, quite imperceptible in coffee, wine, or any other beverage. It is also quite imperceptible to any known method of autopsy."

"Do you mean it is a poison?" cried Alan, very much horrified.

The old man said indifferently. "One might call it a life-cleaner. Lives need cleaning sometimes."

"I want nothing of that sort," said Alan.

"Probably it is just as well," said the old man. "Do you know the price of this? For one teaspoonful, which is sufficient, I ask five thousand dollars. Never less. Not a penny less."

"I hope all your mixtures are not as expensive," said Alan apprehensively.

"Oh dear, no," said the old man. "It would be no good charging that sort of price for a love potion, for example. Young people who need a love potion very seldom have five thousand dollars. Otherwise they would not need a love potion."

"I am glad to hear that," said Alan.

"I look at it like this," said the old man. "Please a customer with one article, and he will come back when he needs another. Even if it is more costly. He will save up for it, if necessary."

"So," said Alan, "you really do sell love potions?"

"It is only when one is in a position to oblige that one can afford to be so confidential." said the old man, reaching for another bottle.

"And these potions," said Alan. "They are not just—just—er."

"Oh, no," said the old man. "Their effects are permanent, and extend far beyond the mere casual impulse. But they include it. Oh, yes they include it. Bountifully, insistently. Everlastingly."

"Dear me!" said Alan. "How very interesting!"

"But consider the spiritual side," said the old man.

"I do, indeed," said Alan.

"For indifference," said the old man, "they substitute devotion. For scorn, adoration. Give one tiny measure of this to the young lady—its flavor is imperceptible in orange juice, soup, or cocktails—and however gay and giddy she is, she will change altogether. She will want nothing but solitude and you."

"I can hardly believe it," said Alan. "She is so fond of parties."

"She will not like them anymore," said the old man. "She will be afraid of the pretty girls you may meet."

"She will actually be jealous?" cried Alan in a rapture "Of me?"

"Yes, she will want to be everything to you."

"She is, already. Only she doesn't care about it."

"She will, when she has taken this. She will care intensely. You will be her sole interest in life."

"Wonderful！" cried Alan.

"She will want to know all you do，" said the old man. "All that has happened to you during the day. Every word of it. She will want to know what you are thinking about，why you smile suddenly，why you are looking sad."

"That is love！" cried Alan.

"Yes，" said the old man. "How carefully she will look after you！ She will never allow you to be tired，to sit in a draught，to neglect your food. If you are an hour late，she will be terrified. She will think you are killed，or that some siren has caught you."

"I can hardly imagine Diana like that！" cried Alan, overwhelmed with joy.

"You will not have to use your imagination，" said the old man.

"And，by the way，since there are always sirens，if by any chance you should，later on，slip a little，you need not worry. She will forgive you，in the end. She will be terribly hurt，of course，but she will forgive you — in the end."

"That will not happen，" said Alan fervently.

"Of course not，" said the old man. "But，if it did，you need not worry. She would never divorce you. Oh，no！ And，of course, she will never give you the least，the very least，grounds for—uneasiness."

"And how much，" said Alan，"is this wonderful mixture？"

"It is not as dear，" said the old man，"as life-cleaner, as I sometimes call it. No. One has to be older than you are, to indulge in that sort of thing. One has to save up for it."

"But the love potion?" said Alan.

"Oh, that," said the old man, opening the drawer in the kitchen table, and taking out a tiny, rather dirty-looking phial. "That is just a dollar."

"I can't tell you how grateful I am," said Alan, watching him fill it.

"I like to oblige," said the old man. "Then customers come back, later in life, when they are better off, and want more expensive things. Here you are. You will find it very effective."

"Thank you again," said Alan. "Good-bye."

"Au revoir," said the man.

你这一生

【德】克里斯蒂安·弗兰克 – 本恩

现在，你躺在棺材里，已经有三天的时间了。你的头枕在白边枕头上，戴着手套的双手叠放着，双目紧闭，嘴巴稍稍向上突起。

我知道你不愿意这样，你想尽快下葬，如果可能的话，死的当天下葬，最迟第二天下葬。你告诉过我，你就是这样埋葬你的父亲的，速度很快，根本没有顾忌那天是星期五。当地人不会选择在星期二和星期五下葬，他们耽于迷信，忌讳这么做，而迷信比任何法律都有效。你也没有解释过如果有人破了这个禁忌会有什么后果，会带来厄运吗？会给谁带来厄运呢？你只说过死者属于死者，不属于活着的人，死亡终结了迷信。

于是，你在星期五埋葬了你的父亲，是为了他，不过，自然也是为了你自己。因为这意味着不必等待远道而来奔丧的家人，不需要为许多亲友安排食宿。人必须接受无法改变的现实，非做不可的事情一定要做，还要做得迅速，但不过分张扬。

你希望你的丧事也照此办理，但他们违背了你的意愿：他们等了三天，把星期五挨过去，把葬礼定在星期六的下午。他们把你的棺材放在棺材架上，在通往你住所的路上拉起了一串串吊丧的白旗和花环，在沿途的树上贴满配有你照片的小讣告（我记得很清楚，那张照片是我在我们的花园里拍的），以此表现他们的哀思。他们尽情铺张，说到底，他们为什么不呢？反正所有的账单都由我来支付。只要你还活着，他们就不敢违逆你的意愿：你的话就是统治整个家族的最高指示。然而，你的意愿随着你的死亡也失去了生命力。

你的棺材停在你的房舍前的棺材架上。假如你能睁开眼睛的话，你会看到那棵番石榴树，这棵树是你的骄傲和欢乐，却被你在院子前面竖起的帐篷掩去了一半。

他们给你穿了件黑色的袍子，没给你穿礼服。黑袍是你多年以前参加宗教仪式的时候穿的，袍子硬硬的，长长的，腰带宽宽的，头饰尖尖的，就像一座塔。那时你正值中年，在寺庙和村里备受尊敬和敬仰。此后，你再也没有穿过这件黑袍，你现在穿着也一定不会舒服。你总是身着白衣主持家族的事务，为衣服上只有你才特许拥有的铜纽扣而自豪，因为这使得你在家族里的那些辅助人员中鹤立鸡群，尽管近来你不像以往那样精心擦拭它们了。你病情严重的时候，穿白裤子也有困难了，于是你请求用白纱笼来代替白裤子。不论怎样，白纱笼不一直是你们国家的国服吗？在某些喜庆的场合，你们的总统不也穿纱笼吗？你穿上纱笼，配上白上衣和一头银发，看起来是那么的威严尊贵，俨然总统。

你的长孙，你的三个孙子中最大的，今年还不到五岁。

他站在棺材前头，神情肃穆，毫不畏惧。中午的天气酷热难当，苍蝇被吸引过来，企图落在你的脸上，他用小手把苍蝇轰走。是别人教他这么做的？也许，这对他来说不过是一个游戏？也许，是出于对他的爱？在此之前，他带着同样肃穆、实在的表情，数过客人们放在盒子里的钱：十卢比，二十卢比，也有五十卢比的纸币。他的父亲在练习本子上录入出捐者的名字和所捐的金额。

　　七个和尚围着你的棺材做成半圆形，他们在诵经，一个接一个大段大段地颂扬你的功德。他们完全有理由这么做，因为你给各种各样的寺庙都布施过大量金钱。寺庙和家族是你生活的两个焦点，对此你念念不忘、呵护备至。有些人认为你必须这样，才能抵消你所犯下的恶行。

　　可我却不相信你会为恶行而辗转反侧，你也不会因为虑及受害人的利益而良心发现。你有着严格的道德标准，可是，你总是用这些标准去要求别人，却从来不用这些标准来要求自己。你从来都没有怀疑过自己，也从来没有怜悯过别人，或许是因为你幼年的艰难岁月早早地教会了你去寻找一切机会，在可能的情况下牢牢地把握机会吧？尽管如此，你的家族仍是村里的旺族之一。

　　你坚信每个人的地位都是命中注定的。你对社会革命不感兴趣。世界不变，人的地位不变，等级规范和制约着人的生活轨道，怜悯是奢侈。布施只是实现个人赎罪的手段，与穷人无缘。

　　我相信，你觉得与寺院以及寺院里的和尚关系非常亲近，因为你是一个虔诚的佛教徒。说到底，不久以前，你曾经打算从俗世隐退，过隐士般的生活。你买了橙色的长袍、香扇，以及其他必备之物（是五件吧？）。你不是把一切细节都跟你的同学兼朋友——寺庙里最年长的和尚商讨过了吗？依据印度的古老传统，人上了年纪以后，着眼于即将到来的死亡，可以抛弃家庭，放弃尘世的一切和物质利益，而彻底地专注于获得智慧和自身的精神财富，像隐士似的隐退，你不是诚心诚意地希望你的生命有一个体面的结局吗？

　　在实施最后的步骤之前，有一年的考验期。你为此把一切都安排妥当了，还跟我详细谈论过。可你还没有得到妻子的认可，而这一切都有赖于此。你是在做完了全部准备工作之后，才迟迟把计划告诉她的。你也预料到她不会轻易接受你离去的想法，但她一直很温柔和顺，所以，你期望她能尊重你的意愿，不会阻拦。然而，事实恰好相反，她发动全家人站在她一边，号召你的姐妹站在她那边。于是，她们来了，在你面前摆出了她们所能想到的所有观点和反对意见。你允许她们说，你听着，你连反驳都不想反驳，就放弃了自己的计划，因为你早就打定主意不为这件事争辩。

于是，这件事就这样不了了之了，你也把那件橙色的袍子送给了你的朋友，那个老和尚。

你对这家寺庙的布施很可能为你赢得了一定程度的影响，也许是得到了一个更为广阔的行使权力的领域。对人、对事的权力——这是你的专长，使得你的声望日隆。当一个人了解了人性的弱点，并且知道怎样利用人们的弱点的时候，当一个人不需要人们的爱的时候，当另一个目标更为重要的时候，人们很容易对这个人产生依赖。

对于你来说，这个所谓的另一个目标就是为家族谋福利，你从未偏离过这个方向，不仅如此，你甚至连后事都计划好了。你知道他们对你依赖的程度，关注他们的未来生活是你的头等大事。他们得到的遗产还包括你对别人可以行使的权力。你最青睐的继承人是最小的女儿的三个儿子。你的大女儿也有一个孩子，是一个女孩，可你几乎提都不提，她从来就没在你的头脑中出现过。

明眼人看到这一切，会得出这样一个结论：你不是一个好人。这也正是许多人的原话。毫无疑问，你是一个投机商和剥削者，一个通过贿赂受益的人，一个通过施以小恩小惠搞奴才小集团的人。别人有难的时候，你以大度的姿态把钱借给别人，似乎是在助人为乐，但此后的每个月却都索要高额利息。你从来不要借债的人还本息，因为债务的本息是你不断获利的源头。人有只顾今天的生活，不对明天的突发事件未雨绸缪的弱点，这也是你的同胞的特征。你知道怎样利用这一弱点，特别是在源源不断的稳定利息能够保障小额定期收入的情况下。作为回报，你的受害者对你唯命是从。事实上，他们甚至还赞颂你，当然，那是在你还活着的时候。你驯服的奴才在任何事情上都对你言听计从，他甚至代你向借债人讨债，结果自己成为不受欢迎的人。

你有一个账本，账本准确地记录了这一切，可是你死以后，我们在你家里没有找到。我估计你预感到自己大限将至，所以一定是把账本传给了女婿，把权力移交给了能够控制孙子继承权的人。可是，我们却在你的房里——我怎么说呢——就是在你侵占的房间里，发现了一瓶我们最好的白兰地。我不相信你会偷着喝酒，喝酒不是你的一个弱点。不过，你了解那些脆弱的贪杯的人，当他们让你高兴的时候，你可以报以少量的酒。此中内幕，我确实知之甚少，但我知道你用香槟当礼物买沉默。这样，你就能镇压反抗你恶行的公开叛乱了。说到底，假如有人送礼物的话，人们都无力拒绝，因为人们一直是受这样的教化长大的：有人做出这种姿态的时候，我们的反应应该是友好的，甚至要微笑，因为在人际关系中，和谐被视为最为重要的因素。所以，笑脸可以买，从而避免冲突。在这种情况下，人们又怎么能够抗拒邪恶呢？

我没有告诉你，因为你年事已高，因为你为这个家族服务多年，还因为你的服务井井有条，无可指责（尽管在这一点上，我们最好不谈忠诚与否的问题）。在我发现你是一个无耻的剥削者之后，继续与你共事是多么的困难。那是一个受害者在逃债的时候转而向我们寻求帮助，那件事发生在若干年前，而你当时正在住院。他欠了一身的债务，不仅欠你的，还欠别人的，而别人突然逼迫他还债。倘若当时你在场的话，他也会向你求助，而这样一来，他就会欠下你更多的债务。在当时的那种情形下，他别无选择，就来找我。于是，一切真相大白了：以前他母亲举行葬礼和他女儿住院治疗需要大笔大笔的钱时，你曾经"帮助"过他，借钱给他，而他多年以来一直在付你利息，月复一月，他付的利息已经远远超过最初所借的数额，而他还在继续付利息。

假如你是一个年轻人，假如你为我们所做的工作不是这样卓有成效的话，我绝对会把你开除。这不是一个唯一的个案，我们还发现了更多的案例，你大吃一惊——自然是对你不利的，我们结算了所有的预付款，同时小心翼翼地保存着你的面子，也保全了那个把此事和盘托出的不幸的人的脸面。

后来，当我恢复了平静，能够更客观地思考问题的时候，我不由得钦佩你蜘蛛般织网的本领。那种不仅了解同胞的问题，而且了解他们的弱点，同时保持着没有同情心态度的人，能够得到更多。你的个性很强，别人的认可与你无关。当你的敲诈勒索是以善意的面目出现时，你沾沾自喜，洋洋得意。你经营的不仅是金钱，还有被你巧取豪夺的他人的尊敬与恐惧。毫无疑问，你可以经常得到雇主的好感。你广博的经历，你完成本职工作时所采用的审慎的、具有预见性的方法，对此都起了决定性的作用。你能够巧妙地把属于其他人的赞扬转嫁过来，你把所有的钱都抓在自己的手里。

我敢肯定你信奉严格的自律，你经历过艰难岁月。为了向热望中的成功迈进，你像年轻人似的工作。你牺牲夜间的睡眠时间学习英语，为了达到自己设定的目标表现出极强的意志品质。与此同时，你认识到，人太宽厚太友善都是错误，信任别人，相信他们有自知之明最终注定会失望。"假如缰绳勒得不够紧，他们就会像疯牛似的发疯，想阻止都阻止不了……"我记得你曾经引述过这个说法，我却难以领悟其中的智慧。我知道这是人格的弱点，这一弱点并不总是带来好的结果。

在去医院动这次非动不可的大手术之前，你准备好了一切后事以防万一，你把一切都安排妥当了。你有两个女儿，你给她俩都留了财产，但只生了一个女孩的长女得到的遗产，比生了三个男孩的次女少得多。次女一直被你视为掌上明珠，在她生了第三个儿子以后，你在家里照顾她，倾注了极大的爱。而当时长女刚刚流产，你却听之任之，不理不睬，尽管这时的她需要更多的关注和安慰。这么做冷酷无情，缺乏人道，同时也是一个错误，因为这造成了家庭成员间的矛盾。而你在这件事的处理上，却没有用智慧来判断人性，也没有预料到自己的所作所为所带来的后果。或许是你不在意，你推测风暴终会过去吧？

如果说你此生有过伟大的爱的话，那就是你对孙子们的爱。在弥留之际，你对妻子说："照顾好我的孙子。"这就是你的最后遗言，只有孙子才是最重要的。

我想你对此事不会太忧心忡忡：那条你的家族以你的名字命名的、通向你的那三幢房子和田地的窄小的巷子，被某个不知名的人换了新路牌，上书："利息巷"，具有报复的意味，在你活着的时候，断断不会有人如此胆大妄为。

除了你自己，谁也没有料到你会死。你有心理准备，你是在鲜血流尽之后死的，一如你让别人流血。

不过，我们还是在你的尸体上洒上圣水。他们盖上棺材抬着它沿着那条路向墓地走去。没有人跟随，没有人哭泣。人们很快就忘了你，即使那些从你身上学到许多东西的人也不例外。

但是，我却无法忘记你，我并不是带着爱意想起你。你是稻田里一块迎风而立的硬石头；你是一棵树，你的树冠遮挡了阳光，你的树根霸占了水源，剥夺了其他树木享受阳光和水分的权利。

我不欣赏你，可我忘不了你。

Testimonial

By Christiane Franke-Benn

Now you lie in your coffin, for three days already. Your head rests on a white lace-edged pillow, and your gloved hands are folded. Your eyes are closed and the mouth protrudes a little.

I know that this is not what you wanted. You wanted to be buried quickly, if possible on the same day you died, or on the next at the latest. You told me that this is how you buried your father, quickly and without considering that it was a Friday. Here the dead are not buried on either Tuesdays or Fridays, superstition does not allow it, and superstition is more powerful than any law. Nor did you explain what would happen if one were to break the taboo. Would it bring bad luck? To whom? All you said was that the dead belong to the dead and not to the living, and that death puts an end to superstition.

And so you buried your father on a Friday, for his sake. But also of course for your sake. For it meant that there was to be no waiting for family members who come traveling from afar, no need for accommodation and food for many relations. One has to accept what cannot be altered, and what has to be done must be done, quickly and without too great a display.

That is how you wanted it for your death too. But they did not heed your wishes: they waited for three days, allowed the Friday to pass and fixed the funeral for Saturday afternoon. They placed your coffin on a bier, and proclaimed their mourning by stringing white flags and garlands along the road leading to your house and pasting small posters with your photograph on trees. (I well remember the day when I took that photograph, in our garden.) They spared no expenses. After all, why should they, since all the bills were sent to me. As long as you lived they dared not ignore your wishes: your word reigned supreme in the family. But your wishes did not survive your death.

Your coffin stands on a bier in front of your house. If you could open your eyes you would see the guava tree which was your pride and joy. But it is half hidden by the tent which has been erected in front of your compound.

They have dressed you in a black suit, not in the garment of honor, the stiff long robe with the broad sash and towering headdress which you wore for a temple procession many years ago, when you were in the middle of your life, respected and honored by both temple and village. This black suit you have never worn and you would not have felt comfortable in it. Dressed in white you presided over our household, proud of the brass buttons on your jacket which only your were allowed to have and which distinguished you from all the other helpers in the house, even if lately you did not give so much attention to polishing them as earlier. When the illness became more troublesome it was difficult for you to wear the White trousers, and so you asked for permission to exchange it for a white sarong. In any case, isn't that the national dress of your country? Doesn't even the President of your country wear a white sarong on festive occasions? You also looked like a president, so dignified in your white sarong and white jacket, and with your white hair.

Your grandchild, the eldest of the three small brothers, is not more than five years old.

He stands at the head of the coffin, his face serious and unafraid, and watches the flies which, attracted by the midday heat try to settle on your face. He uses his small hand to chase them away. Did anyone ask him to do this? Or is it a game for him? Or perhaps it is love? In the same serious and matter-of-fact manner he had earlier counted the money which visitors place in a box: ten, twenty and sometimes fifty rupee notes. His father enters both the amount and the name of the donor in an exercise book.

Seven Buddhist monks sit in a semi-circle round your coffin. They chant sutras and then, one by one, they make long speeches praising your good deeds. They have reason for this, for you have donated a great deal of money to the various temples. The temple and your family, those were the two focal points of your life. They were always in your thoughts and you took good care of them. There are those who believe that it was necessary for you to do this to balance the account of your evil deeds.

But I do not believe that you lost any sleep over any of the wicked things you did, nor that your conscience was burdened by the thought of them. You had strict moral standards but you used these only to measure others by, never yourself. You never had doubts about yourself, nor pity for others. Maybe a hard time experienced as a child taught you early to look but for opportunities and to grasp them wherever possible? And yet your family was among the most prosperous in the village.

You were also convinced that everyone's status is determined by birth. Social revolution did not interest you. Where the world is to remain unchanged, where status is unalterable and the rules of caste determine the course of one's life, pity is a luxury. The giving of alms serves only the achievement of personal redemption, and poverty has no chance.

I believe that you felt close to the temple and its clergy because you were really a convinced Buddhist. After all, it is not so very long ago that you decided to withdraw from the world and enter the priesthood. You had already bought the orange-color robe, the fan, and the other (Is it five?) necessary items. And had you not discussed all this with your friend the most senior monk in your temple with whom you had gone to school? Was it not really your wish to achieve a dignified ending to your life, quite in the old Indian tradition where, with increasing age a man may retreat to live as a hermit, forsaking the family and giving up all worldly and material concerns, concentration entirely on the acquisition of wisdom and one's own spiritual welfare, with a view to the approaching end?

There was to be a one year's trial before the final step was taken. You had made all arrangements towards this, and you and I talked about it at length. But you had still not obtained your wife's agreement, and everything depended on that. You postponed telling her about your plan until you had completed all the preparations. You probably knew that she would not accept your going lightly, but she had always been gentle and subservient and you must have hoped that she would respect your wishes and offer no resistance. Instead she alerted the whole family, called your sisters to her side, and they came and placed before all the arguments and recriminations they could think of. You allowed them to have their say and you listened. And without any attempt to counter their arguments you abandoned your plan. Because you had made up your mind earlier that you would not fight for it.

So it all came to nothing. The orange-colored robe you gave to your friend, the monk.

It is also possible that your donations to the temple achieved for you a degree of influence, maybe a wider field to exercise your power. Power—both over people and things—that was your speciality and ongoing fame. It is easy to make people dependent when one knows their weaknesses and how to exploit them, and when one does not need their affection, when another objective is more important.

For you, this objective was the welfare of your family. You never lost sight of that, and planned beyond your death. You knew to what extent they depended on you and that your care for their later life was of the utmost importance. Their inheritance should also include the power you wielded over others. And the preferred inheritors were your youngest daughter's three sons. That your other daughter also has a child, a girl, you hardly mentioned. She was never in your thoughts.

When one looks at all this with a clear eye one comes to the conclusion that you were not a good human being. There are many who say precisely that. Without question, you were a profiteer and exploiter, one who through bribery obtains favors, and who through giving favors creates a côterie of slaves. You have lent money with a grand gesture, appearing to help in case of need, and then charged massive interest every month. You never asked your debtors to repay the capital, because the capital became a constant source of income for you. People have a weakness to live only for the day and not to prepare for emergencies. This is a characteristic of your land and this weakness you knew how to exploit, especially in cases where a small regular income insured a steady flow of interest. In return your victims did whatever you wished them to. In fact, they even praised you, that is, while you were alive. Your most obedient slave obeyed you in all matters. He even collected money from your debtors for you and became unpopular as a result.

You kept precise accounts of all this. These accounts were not to be found in our house after you died. I assume that as you anticipated your death you must have passed them on to your son-in-law, handing over the power to the man who was to control the inheritance for the grandsons. Instead we found a bottle of our best brandy in your room which—how shall I put it — you had appropriated. I don't believe that you yourself drank secretly; that was not one of your weaknesses. But you knew those who were weak and who like to drink, and whom you could reward with a nip when they had pleased you. I know only very little of what went on with certainty. But I know that you made presents of our Champagne in order to buy silence. Thus you were able to suppress open rebellion against your misdeeds. After all, how can one deal with wickedness when one is offered a gift and is too weak to refuse, when one has been brought up to react with friendliness to such a gesture, even with a smile, because harmony is considered the most important ingredient in human relations. And so one can buy a smile and avoid confrontation.

I did not tell you because you were old, because you had served so many years in this house, and because your services were of a high order and beyond reprimand（although we had better not talk about loyalty at this point）how difficult it was to continue working with you after I discovered what a shameless exploiter you were. One of your victims had to turn to us in his plight. This was some years ago when you were in the hospital. He was heavily indebted, not only to you but also to others, and these others suddenly pressed for repayment. Had you been there he would have asked you for help, and his debt to you would have increased. Under the circumstances he saw no alternative and came to me. And then everything came to light: he had needed money because his mother's funeral and daughter's treatment in the hospital had cost a great deal. You had "helped" him, lent him money and he had been paying you interest for years, month after month, and what he paid in interest far exceeded the original amount lent. Yet he had to continue to pay interest.

Had you been a young man and had you been less efficient in your work for us, there is no question but I would have dismissed you. And this was not the only case; we discovered many more. You were surprised — and of course, it was not to your advantage—when we settled all outstanding monies. At the same time we took care to save face for you, and also for the unhappy man who had given the whole story away.

Later, when I had recovered my equanimity and was able to think more objectively I could not but admire how you had spun your spider's net. He who not only knows the problems of his fellowmen but also their weaknesses and who can remain free from pity, he can achieve a great deal. You had a strong character. Approbation did not matter to you, although you felt pleased and flattered when your extortions appeared as kindnesses. What you dealt in was not just money; it was the respect and fear of those whom you robbed.

No doubt it was always possible for you to obtain the goodwill of your employers. Your wide experience, your careful and anticipatory method of fulfilling your duties contributed decisively to this. But you were also very adroit at accepting praise that others should have earned. You held all the strings in your hand.

I am sure you believed in firm discipline. You yourself had known bad times, had worked hard as a young man towards the success you craved. You sacrificed your sleep at night in order to learn English, and exerting great willpower achieved the objectives you set yourself. At the same time you knew that it is a mistake to be too lenient or friendly. To trust others and believe that they know their limitations is bound to lead to disappointment. "If one hold the reins too loosely, they run wild, like mad bulls and there will be no end to it..." I remember you quoting this saying, but I find it difficult to accept its wisdom. I know this is a weakness which does not always lead to the best results.

Before you entered the hospital to undergo this serous operation which had become necessary and unavoidable you settled all your affairs, prepared everything in case you were to die. You had two daughters. You made provision for both of them. But the elder of the two who has only one daughter received much less than the younger one who has three sons. This was the one whom you had always spoiled. After the birth of her third child you cared for her in your house with great love and affection. The elder daughter, who had a miscarriage at this time, was left to her own devices although she needed extra attention and reassurance. That was hard and inhuman. It was also a mistake because it created problems in the family. You did not, on this occasion, have the wisdom to judge human nature, nor the consequences of your action. Perhaps you did not care and assumed that the storm would pass?

If you had one great love in your life it was love for your grandsons. "Take care of my sons," you said to your wife as you were about to die. Those were your last words. Only that was important.

I do not think it would have worried you unduly that the narrow pathway which leads to your three houses and your fields, which was named after you by your family, was given a new name board by a person unknown. On it was written "Interest Lane". A revenge of sorts, but only to be risked after your death.

Nobody had expected you to die. Only you. And you were prepared. You bled to death, just as you allowed others to bleed.

Nevertheless, we sprinkle your dead body with holy water. They close the coffin and carry it down the pathway to the burial place. Nobody follows. Nobody cries. They forget you quickly, even those who have learned a great deal from you.

But I cannot forget you, not that I think of you with affection.

You were a hard rock in a paddy field stirred by the wind. You were a tree whose roots deprive other plants from obtaining water and whose crowns deprive them of light.

I do not admire you. But I cannot forget you.

我为什么当老师

【美】皮特·G.贝德勒

你为什么当老师？我告诉我的朋友我不想做行政人员时，他大惑不解，问了我这个问题。所有的美国人被教育所灌输的都是在长大以后追求金钱和权力，而去做一个行政人员显然是"上了一个台阶"。

我当老师自然不是因为教书对于我来说易如反掌。在我尝试过的几种谋生行当——当机械师、木匠和作家中，当老师是最难的。对于我来说，老师这个职业就意味着红红的眼睛、汗津津的手心和沉甸甸的心。红红的眼睛是因为不论我熬夜备课到几点，上课之前还是会觉得准备得不够充分。汗津津的手是因为我进教室之前总是忐忑不安，觉得自己一定会出丑露馅。沉甸甸的心是因为我离开教室一小时以后就会相信自己这次讲得比平时还要枯燥。

我教书也不是因为我善于答疑解惑，也不是因为我知识渊博，驱使我一定得与人分享不可。有的时候，看到学生上我的课记笔记，我还很吃惊呢！

那么，我，为什么偏偏当老师呢？

我当老师是因为我喜欢学校的节奏。六月、七月和八月这三个假期提供了反思、研究和写作的机会。

我当老师是因为老师是一个建筑在变化之上的职业。虽然教科书还是原来的教科书，我却发生了改变，更重要的是，我的学生也发生了改变。

我喜欢教书是因为我有犯错误的自由，吸取教训的自由，激励自己和学生的自由。作为一个教师，我的地盘我做主。假如我要新生自己编课本，作为学习写作的途径，谁又能管得着？也许这样的课程可能彻底失败，不过我们都能从失败中习得知识。

我当老师是因为我喜欢向学生提需要绞尽脑汁才能回答出来的问题。这个世界上到处都是蹩脚问题的正确答案，在教书的过程中，我有时会发现高明的问题。

我当老师是因为我可以找到让我和学生们走出象牙塔，进入现实世界的途径。我曾经教过一门名叫《在技术社会自立》的课程。我的十五名学生读爱默生、梭罗和赫胥黎的作品。他们坚持记日记。他们写学期论文。

不过，我们还创建了一个公司，贷款买了一幢被撞倒的房子，我们通过整修房子锻炼自立的能力。期末的时候，我们把房子卖掉，还清了贷款，纳了税，小组成员分了红。

所以，教书给我的生活带来了节奏、多样化、挑战，以及不断学习的机会。

哦，我漏掉了我教书最重要的原因。

一个原因是维姬。维姬是我指导的第一个博士生，她精力充沛，殚精竭虑地撰写一篇长篇学术论文，详细分析一位籍籍无名的十四世纪的诗人。她撰写文章，往学术期刊投递。她独立完成这一切，我只是偶尔督促督促她而已。可是，她完成论文的时候我在场，听说她投递的论文已经发表，她得到了一份工作，还与哈佛合作编书，把她刚刚做我的学生时所萌发的思想写进书里。

另一个原因是乔治。他开始是学工程的，后来转到了英语专业，因为他渐渐明白自己爱人胜过爱物。

还有珍妮。珍妮大学中途辍学，可是她的同学要她看自力更生整修的工程完工的景象，把她拉了回来。她回来的时候，我也在场。她告诉我她后来对城市贫民问题产生了兴趣，所以后来做了维护公民权的代理律师。

还有雅基。雅基是一个保洁员，她凭知觉知道的比我们大多数人凭借分析所学到的还要多。雅基决定完成高中学业然后进大学深造。

以上是我选择当老师的真正原因，我目睹了这些人在我面前成长变化。当老师就是在创造天地的时候，在泥土开始呼吸的时候在场。

不当老师的"晋升"会给我带来金钱和权力。可是现在也有钱，我还可以带薪做自己喜欢的事情：读书，与人交谈，问诸如此类的问题，"富裕的意义何在？"

我还有权力。我有权去启迪，去激发才智，去开列参考书目，去指点迷津。其他权力哪有这样的权力影响深远？

当老师还会带来超越金钱和权力的东西：那就是爱。不仅仅是对学习、书籍、思想的爱，还有当出类拔萃的学生走进老师的生活开始呼吸成长的时候，老师所感觉到的爱。也许用"爱"这个词不合适，用"魔力"可能更恰当。

我当老师是因为，活在开始呼吸成长的人中间，我有时会发觉自己与他们同呼吸，共成长。

Why I Teach

By Peter G. Beidler

Why do you teach? My friend asked the question when I told him that I didn't want to be considered for an administrative position. He was puzzled that I did not want what was obviously a "step up" toward what all Americans are taught to want when they grow up: money and power.

Certainly I don't teach because teaching is easy for me. Teaching is the most difficult of the various ways I have attempted to earn my living: mechanic, carpenter, writer. For me, teaching is a red-eye, sweaty-palm, sinking-stomach profession. Red-eye, because I never feel ready to teach no matter how late I stay up preparing. Sweaty-palm, because I'm always nervous before I enter the classroom, sure that I will be found out for the fool that I am. Sinking-stomach, because I leave the classroom an hour later convinced that I was even more boring than usual.

Nor do I teach because I think I know answers, or because I have knowledge I feel compelled to share. Sometimes I am amazed that my students actually take notes on what I say in class!

Why, then, do I teach?

I teach because I like the pace of the academic calendar. June, July, and August offer an opportunity for reflection, research and writing.

I teach because teaching is a profession built on change. When the material is the same, I change—and, more important, my students change.

I teach because I like the freedom to make my own mistakes, to learn my own lessons, to stimulate myself and my students. As a teacher, I'm my own boss. If I want my freshmen to learn to write by creating their own textbook, who is to say I can't? Such courses may be huge failures, but we can all learn from failures.

I teach because I like to ask questions that students must struggle to answer. The world is full of right answers to bad questions. While teaching, I sometimes find good questions.

I teach because I enjoy finding ways of getting myself and my students out of the ivory tower and into the real world. I once taught a course called "Self-Reliance in a Technological Society." My 15 students read Emerson, Thoreau, and Huxley. They kept diaries. They wrote term papers.

But we also set up a corporation, borrowed money, purchased a run-down house and practiced self-reliance by renovating it. At the end of the semester, we sold the house, repaid our loan, paid our taxes, and distributed the profits among the group.

So teaching gives me pace, and variety, and challenge, and the opportunity to keep on learning.

I have left out, however, the most important reasons why I teach.

One is Vicky. My first doctoral student, Vicky was an energetic student who labored at her dissertation on a little-known 14th century poet. She wrote articles and sent them off to learned journals. She did it all herself, with an occasional nudge from me. But I was there when she finished her dissertation, learned that her articles were accepted, got a job and won a fellowship to Harvard working on a book developing ideas she'd first had as my student.

Another reason is George, who started as an engineering student, then switched to English because he decided he liked people better than things.

There is Jeanne, who left college, but was brought back by her classmates because they wanted her to see the end of the self-reliance house project. I was there when she came back. I was there when she told me that she later became interested in the urban poor and went on to become a civil rights lawyer.

There is Jacqui, a cleaning woman who knows more by intuition than most of us learn by analysis. Jacqui has decided to finish high school and go to college.

These are the real reasons I teach, these people who grow and change in front of me. Being a teacher is being present at the creation, when the clay begins to breathe.

A "promotion" out of teaching would give me money and power. But I have money. I get paid to do what I enjoy: reading, talking with people, and asking questions like, "What is the point of being rich?"

And I have power. I have the power to nudge, to fan sparks, to suggest books, to point out a pathway. What other power matters?

But teaching offers something besides money and power: it offers love. Not only the love of learning and of books and ideas, but also the love that a teacher feels for that rare student who walks into a teacher's life and begins to breathe. Perhaps love is the wrong word: magic might be better.

I teach because, being around people who are beginning to breathe, I occasionally find myself catching my brea with them.

书与友谊

通常情况下，欲了解一个人的为人，可以看他交什么样的朋友，也可以看他读什么样的书。因为人可以与人为友，也可以与书结谊。不仅如此，不论择友还是择书，我们均应择善而从。

一本好书可能会成为最好的朋友。它不论过去、现在，还是将来，都忠贞不渝。是最有耐心、最令人愉悦的朋友。它不会在我们患难和痛苦时背弃我们，相反，它会自始至终永远善意地接纳我们。我们青春年少时，书给予我们教益和欢乐；我们白发苍苍时，书给予我们享受和慰藉。

我们常常会发现，两个人由于热爱同一本书结下了友谊，正如两个人由于倾慕第三者结下的友谊。古谚有云："爱吾，则爱吾之犬。"

此谚若改成"爱我，就爱我的书。"的话，岂不更有智慧？书是人与人之间更真挚、更崇高的纽带。借由人们共同挚爱的作家，人们可以相互想象、感知和怜悯。读者活在作者的心中，作者也活在读者的心中。

书引导我们进入最优秀的朋友圈；让我们面对历朝历代的伟人，仿佛他们依然健在，仿佛可以听其言，观其行，见其人。我们与他们同悲悯，共喜悲。他们的经验经历成为我们的经验经历。在某种程度上，我们感觉仿佛与书中所描绘的人物一道在舞台上粉墨登场了。

书虽死物，在我们的生命里，却是活的声音，与友无异。

Companionship of Books

A man may usually be known by the books he reads as well as by the company he keeps; for there is a companionship of books as well as men; and one should always live in the best company, whether it be of books or of men.

A good book may be among the best friends. It is the same today that it always was, and it will never change. It is the most patient and cheerful of companions. It does not turn its back upon us in time of adversity or distress. It always receives us with the same kindness; amusing and instructing us in youth, and comforting and consoling us age.

Men often discover their affinity to each other by the love they have each other for a book—just as two persons sometimes discover a fiend by the admiration which both have for a third. There is an old proverb, "Love me, love my dog."

But there is more wisdom in this: "Love me, love my book." The book is truer and higher bond of union. Men can think, feel, and sympathize with each other through their favorite author. They live in him together, and he in them.

　　Books introduce us into the best society; they bring us into the presence of the greatest minds that have ever lived. We hear what they said and did; we see them as if they were alive; we sympathize with them, enjoy with them, grieve with them; their experiences becomes ours, and we feel as if we were in a measure actors with them in the scenes which they describes.

　　A book is a living voice, just as a friend in our lives.

想要有个家

人人都需要家：孩子认为父母的家就是自己的家；寄宿学生在上学的那五天里，把学校称为"家"；新婚夫妇同心协力建造新家；而旅人呢……至少要有几个晚上在没有可以称为"家"的地方客居。

而那些必须羁旅更久的旅人，他们是怎么解无家可归之苦的呢？莫非他们就没有拥有家的权利吗？他们肯定有啊。

一些常常离家在外的旅客会携带诸如床单、枕套和家人照片等日用品，这样一来，不论身在何方，都会创造出如家的感觉；有些人会选择长期住在某家旅馆，一来二去，对旅馆的服务和服务员都熟悉起来，以此创造出如家的感觉；另一些人索性在宾馆的窗台上摆放鲜花，进一步创造家的环境和感觉。更有登峰造极的人，他们自驾露营车去旅游，晚上就在露营车里睡觉，与居家一模一样——只不过这个家是可以移动的哦！

那么，那些在羁旅中辗转的人，他们又是怎样与他人保持联系的呢？一些人通过因特网与友人联系；一些人邮寄信件、明信片，甚至照片给他人；另一些人只是简单打电话问个好，仅仅是为了让朋友们知道他们不仅还活着，而且活得还挺好。人人都想方设法地与他人保持联系。在旅途中交朋友，或多或少可以让人有家的感觉。青年旅馆里的背包客可能会成为比兄弟姐妹还要亲的密友。

今天，人们大多身在异乡工作打拼，他们又是怎样创造归属感的呢？每当我们背井离乡，前方总会有另一个"家"有待我们去发现。不论身在何方，只要展开一点点想象力，做一点点努力，我们就能够把我们的漂泊之地变身为"家"。

Home on the Way

People need homes: children assume their parents' place as home; boarders call school "home" on weekdays; married couples work together to build new homes; and travelers… have no place to call "home", at least for a few nights.

So how about people who have to travel for extended periods of time? Don't they have the right to a home? Of course they do.

Some regular travelers take their own belongings: like bed sheets, pillowcases and family photos to make them feel like home no matter where they are; some stay for long periods in the same hotel and as a result become very familiar with service and attendants; others may simply put some flowers by the hotel window to make things more homely. Furthermore, driving a camping car during one's travels and sleeping in the vehicle at night is just like home—only mobile!

And how about maintaining relationships while in transit? Some keep contact with their friends via internet; some send letters and postcards, or even photos; others may just call and say hi, just to let their friends know that they're still alive and well. People find ways to keep in touch. Making friends on the way helps travelers feel more or less at home. Backpackers in youth hostels may become very good friends, even closer than siblings.

Nowadays, fewer people are working in their local towns, so how do they develop a sense of belonging? Whenever we step out of our local boundaries, there is always another "home" waiting to be found. Wherever we are, with just a little bit of effort and imagination, we can make the place we stay "home".

母亲的苹果

　　人的早期教育来自家庭，特别是他或者她的母亲。美国一位著名心理学家为了研究母亲对孩子一生的影响，在全美遴选出 50 位成功人士，以及 59 名有过作奸犯科记录的人，请他们谈谈母亲对他们的影响。

　　有两封回信给他留下的印象最为深刻：一封是白宫的一位名人写的，一封是一个被收监服刑的犯人写的。他们写的都是同一件事：小时候母亲给他们分苹果的故事。

　　监狱的犯人在信中写道：

　　小时候，有一天，妈妈拿来几个苹果，有红有绿，大小不同。我特别想要其中最红最大的那个。这时，妈妈把苹果都放到了桌子上，问我和弟弟："你们想要哪个？"我正想说要最大最红的那个，弟弟却抢先说出了我的心里话。妈妈听了，瞪了他一眼，责备道："好孩子要学会把好东西让给别人，而不是自私自利。"我随机应变，改口道："妈妈，我想要那个最小的，最大的应该留给弟弟！"妈妈听了喜出望外，在我的脸上亲了一下，把那个又红又大的苹果奖励给了我。

　　我说了谎，却得到了我想要的东西，就这样，我从此学会了说谎。以后，我又学会了打架、偷盗、抢劫。我为了得到想要的东西，不择手段。所以后来，我就被关进了监狱。

白宫的名人在信中这样写道：

　　小时候，有一天妈妈拿来几个苹果，有红有绿，大小不同。我和两个弟弟都想要最大的那个，妈妈拿起那个最大的苹果对我们说："都想得到这个最大的苹果，很好。现在，就让我们来一个竞赛，我把家门前的草坪分成三部分，你们每个人负责一部分。去修剪草坪，谁干得最快最好，就把最大的苹果奖励给谁。"最后，我赢得了那个苹果。

　　我非常感谢母亲，因为她教会了我一个最基本，然而也是最重要的道理：要想得到最好的，就必须奋勇争先。她一直用这种方法教育我们，我们也是一直遵从教诲。在我们家里，你想要什么，都要通过竞赛来赢取。这很公平：你想要什么，想要多少，就必须为此付出多少努力和代价。

摇摇篮的手，也是撼动世界的手。母亲是孩子的第一任教师，你既可以教他说第一句谎话，也可以教他做一个诚实的、奋勇争先的人。

Mother's Apple

One's education started from family, especially his or her mother. There was a renowned psychologist in America who had done a study on the impact of mother on her children's lives. He singled out 50 successful people in America and 59 people with criminal records and asked them to talk about the influence their mothers had exerted on them.

There are two letters impressing him most. One is from a famous celebrity from the White House while the other from a prisoner in jail. Both of them talked about the same thing in the letters: the story of their mothers' distributing apples to them.

Here is the story from the prisoner:

When I was young, one day my mother brought several apples of different colors and sizes, among which there was a biggest red one that I was eager to get. At that time, my mum put all the apples on the table and asked me and my younger brother,

"Which do you like?" I was about to say "the biggest one"

while my brother took one step ahead and said what I wanted to say. My mum glared at him and blamed him by saying, "A good child should know to give the best to others instead of being self-centered." My learnt a quick lesson and said to my mum, "Mum, I would like the smallest one. The biggest one should be left for my brother!" At hearing my words, my mum felt more than happy and kissed my cheek, giving the biggest apple to me as a reward.

I told a lie but I got what I wanted by doing it. Since then, I learnt to lie. Later, I learnt to fight, steal and rob. I would try all means to get what I wanted. Then later I was put behind bars.

Here is the story from the celebrity:

When I was young, one day my mum brought several apples of different colors and sizes. Both my two younger brothers and I wanted the biggest one. My mum picked up the biggest apple and said to us, "It is good to get the biggest apple. Now let's start a competition. I will divide the lawn in front of our house into three parts, each of you responsible for one respectively. Who could prune his own share of lawn the best and the quickest will be rewarded with the biggest apple." I won the apple finally.

I feel very grateful to my mum because she taught me a very basic but significant wisdom: If you want to get the best, you *must compete to be the No.1. She has been teaching us in this way and we followed her advice all the time. At my home, I needed to compete for what I wanted. It is quite fair because what and how much you want should be acquired with equivalent effort and cost.*

The hand rocking the cradle is the one promoting the world. Mother is the first teacher of children, who can teach them to tell the first lie or teach them to be an honest and No.1-pursuing person.

魔法大衣

在马萨诸塞州北安普顿市的一家出售二手服装的商店里，我和14岁的儿子约翰同时盯上了那件大衣。大衣就挂在衣架上，混在劣质军用风雨衣和各式各样寒酸的羊毛大衣中间，宛若荆棘丛中的一朵玫瑰那样夺人眼球。

其他的大衣都显得垂头丧气的，唯独这件衣服显得神气活现。这件双排扣暗钮长大衣显然还没上过身，厚厚的黑色羊毛柔软而蓬松，看上去就像铺上了樟脑球在已故的老亨利伯伯的扁平旅行箱里保存了多年的样子。大衣做工精美：领子是黑天鹅绒的，商标是第五大道的，仅售28美元，性价比高得令人难以置信。我们默默地交换了一下眼色，而约翰的眼睛已经亮了。黑色的羊毛轻便大衣当时在十几岁的男孩中间是潮物，可是要买件新的却需要花费几百美元，而这一件质地更好一些，还带有一丝复古风和古典美。

约翰将胳膊伸进了厚实的绸缎里子袖筒里，系上了扣子。他转来转去，审视着镜子里的自己，先是一脸的严肃，随即一脸的笑意。衣服与人珠联璧合，浑然一体。

约翰次日就穿着大衣上学去了，放学回来时笑容满面。"孩子们觉得你的大衣怎么样？"我问他。"他们非常喜欢。"他一边说，一边仔仔细细把衣服叠起来搭在椅背上，用手抚平。我就开始叫他"切斯特菲尔德大人"和"了不起的盖茨比"。

在接下来的几个星期里，约翰身上发生了微妙的变化：不再逆反而是听话，不再强词夺理而是心平气和，有商有量。他变得通情达理、彬彬有礼，周到体贴，愿意取悦别人，每天晚上都会说："妈妈，晚饭真好吃。"他会慷慨大方地把自己的磁带借给弟弟，还教育他举止得体，行为规范；他会二话不说，把烧炉子用的劈柴抱进来。有一天，我建议他在晚饭前开始做作业，约翰这个习惯拖拖拉拉的家伙竟然回答："您说得对，我想我会的。"

当我对他的一个老师提起这一突变，说我不知道是什么原因导致的，她朗声大笑，答道："肯定是因为他那件大衣啦！"另一个老师告诉他，她要给他一个高分，不仅仅因为他题答得好，还因为她喜欢他的大衣。在图书馆，我们碰巧碰到了一个朋友，他已经很长时间没有见过我的孩子约翰了。他仰起头来看着约翰，吃惊地问道："这是约翰吗？"他发现约翰个子长高了，他品评着约翰大衣的做工剪裁，还像一个绅士对待另一个绅士那样伸出了手。

我和约翰都明白，我们绝对不应该以貌取人，可是，穿着优雅让别人赏心悦目，在思想上、言语上、行动上践行优秀的标准，内外兼修，也同样值得推崇。

有时，看着约翰去上学，我不由得忆起自己上八年级时的感觉，心中有一种强烈的剧痛——那时，尝试不同的生活途径易如反掌，就像尝试一件衣服一样。整个世界、整个未来在你面前展开，犹如一幅巨大的画卷，画卷里门扉洞开。倘若此时此刻我能回到从前，我会想象自己穿着我奇妙的魔法大衣在这些门中间进进出出，穿行自如。

The Magical Coat

My 14-year-old son, John, and I spotted the coat simultaneously. It was hanging on a rack at a secondhand clothing store in Northampton Mass, crammed in with shoddy trench coats and an assortment of sad, woolen overcoats—a rose among thorns.

While the other coats drooped, this one looked as if it were holding itself up. The thick, black wool of the double-breasted chesterfield was soft and unworn, as though it had been preserved in mothballs for years in dead old Uncle Henry's steamer trunk. The coat had a black velvet collar, beautiful tailoring, a Fifth Avenue label and an unbelievable price of $28. We looked at each other, saying nothing, but John's eyes gleamed. Dark, woolen topcoats were popular just then with teenage boys, but could cost several hundred dollars new. This coat was even better, bearing that touch of classic elegance from a bygone era.

John slid his arms down into the heavy satin lining of the sleeves and buttoned the coat. He turned from side to side, eyeing himself in the mirror with a serious, studied expression that soon changed into a smile. The fit was perfect.

John wore the coat to school the next day and came home wearing a big grin. "How did the kids like your coat?" I asked. "They loved it," he said, carefully folding it over the back of a chair and smoothing it flat. I started calling him "Lord Chesterfield" and "The Great Gatsby".

Over the next few weeks, a change came over John. Agreement replaced contrariness, quiet, reasoned discussion replaced argument. He became more judicious, more mannerly, more thoughtful, eager to please. "Good dinner, Mom," he would say every evening. He would generously loan his younger brother his tapes and lecture him on the niceties of behaviour; without a word of objection, he would carry in wood for the stove. One day when I suggested that he might start on homework before dinner, John—a veteran procrastinator said, "You're right. I guess I will."

When I mentioned this incident to one of his teachers and remarked that I didn't know what caused the changes, she said laughing. "It must be his coat!" Another teacher told him she was giving him a good mark not only because he had earned it but because she liked his coat. At the library, we ran into a friend who had not seen our children in a long time, "Could this be John?" he asked, looking up to John's new height, assessing the cut of his coat and extending his hand, one gentleman to another.

John and I both know we should never mistake a person's clothes for the real person within them. But there is something to be said for wearing a standard of excellence for the world to see, for practising standards of excellence in thought, speech, and behaviour, and for matching what is on the inside to what is on the outside.

Sometimes, watching John leave for school, I've remembered with a keen sting what it felt like to be in the eighth grade—a time when it was as easy to try on different approaches to life as it was to try on a coat. The whole world, the whole future is stretched out ahead, a vast panorama where all the doors are open. And if I were there right now, I would picture myself walking through those doors wearing my wonderful, magical coat.

四季梨树

从前有一个人，他有四个儿子。他轮番派他们到一个遥远的地方去观察一棵梨树。

他们去的季节各不相同：大儿子是在寒冷的冬日，二儿子是在温暖的春天，老三是在炎炎的夏日，最小的儿子是在金色的秋天。他们去了，他们回来了。父亲把他们叫到一起，听他们讲一下他们的所见所闻。

大儿子批评说梨树树枝弯曲，体弱多病，形象丑陋。二儿子连忙反驳并非如此，相反，梨树满树嫩绿的新芽，生机盎然。老三更说满树梨花，竞相开放，那么美，那么香。最小的儿子无法认同所有哥哥的说法，他说梨树上硕果累累，收获多多，香甜可口，生机勃勃。

听了儿子们的叙述，父亲说，他们的说法都没有错，因为他们看到的是大树生命年轮中四个季节里的四个不同的景象。他告诉他们，看树不能看一季，看人不能看一时，因为生命的本质是——生命生发出的喜、乐、爱，而这些，只有在生命完结的时候，方能公正评说。

倘若你在冬季就已放弃，你无疑会错过春季的勃勃生机，夏季的芬芳美丽，以及秋季的累累硕果，所以，切勿为一季的痛苦而破坏了其余三季的欢乐。

Four Seasons of a Tree

There was a man. He had four sons. He wanted his sons to go and look at a pear tree that was far away.

The first son went in the winter, the second in the spring the third in summer, the youngest son in fall. when they had all gone and come back, he called them together to describe what they had seen.

The first son said that the tree was ugly, bent and weak. the second son said no—it was covered with green buds and full of promise. the third son said it was laden with blossoms and they smelt so sweet and looked so beautiful. the last son disagreed with all of them, he said it was ripe and droop with fruit, full of life and fulfillment.

The man then said to his sons that they were all right, because they each had seen but only one season in the tree's life. He told them that they cannot judge a tree or a person, by only one season, and that the essence of who they are—the pleasure, the joy and love that come from that life—can only be measured at the end, when all the seasons are up.

If you give up when it is winter, you will miss the promise of your spring, the beauty of your summer, the fulfillment of your fall. don't let the pain of one season destroy the joy of all the rest.

我们都是破罐子

印度有一个挑水工，他有两个挑水用的大罐子，一个有裂缝，另一个却完美无瑕。挑水工用一根棍子把两个罐子挂在两头挑在肩上，从小河到主人家长长的路上，好罐子能带回满满一罐水，破罐子到家只剩半罐水了。

两年来，挑水工每天都挑着一罐半水到主人家。自然，那只完美无瑕的罐子对自己的成功感到志得意满，觉得物尽其用；而可怜的破罐子自惭形秽，对于只能完成一半任务感到痛苦异常。在两年痛苦和失败的煎熬过后，破罐子在河边对挑水工说："我为自己感到羞愧，我想向你道歉。"

"为什么？"挑水工问道，"你有什么好羞愧的？"

"在过去的两年里，我每天只能带回半罐水，我侧翼的裂缝走一路漏一路，一直漏到你主人家。由于我的缺陷，你这么辛苦劳作，却不能体现你的全部价值。"破罐子解释道。

挑水人为破罐子感到难过，出于同情，他安慰它："我们回主人家的路上，请你注意路边美丽的鲜花。"确实如此，他们爬上小山的时候，破罐子注意到阳光温暖着路边美丽的野花，这让它高兴了些。

可是，在到达目的地的时候，看到漏得只剩半罐水了，它还是感觉好不起来，于是它再次为自己的无能向挑水人道歉。挑水人却对它说：

"你只注意到你那一侧有野花,却没有注意另一侧吧？我了解你的缺陷，所以利用了你的缺陷，在你那一侧种下了花籽，这样，我们每天从河边回来，你就可以浇花了。两年来，我一直在摘那些美丽的花朵来装点主人的餐桌。没有你的裂缝，他哪来扮美他家的鲜花？"

我们每个人都有独一无二的缺陷，我们都是破罐子。不要为你的缺陷而自惭。承认自己的缺陷，你也可以成为美之源。要知道，我们的弱项也是我们的强项。

The Cracked Pot

A water bearer in India had two large pots, each hung on each end of a pole which he carried across his neck. One of the pots had a crack in it, and while the other pot was perfect and always delivered a full portion of water at the end of the long walk from the stream to the master's house, the cracked pot arrived only half full.

For two years this went on daily, with the water bearer delivering one and one-half pots full of water to his masters house. Of course, the perfect pot was proud of its accomplishments, perfect for the purpose for which it was made. But the poor cracked pot was ashamed of its own imperfection, and miserable that it was able to accomplish only half of what it had been made to do. After two years of what it had perceived to be bitter failure, it spoke one day to the water bearer by the stream. "I am ashamed of myself, and I want to apologize to you."

"Why?" asked the bearer. "What are you ashamed of?"

"I have been able for these last two years to deliver only half my load, because this crack in my side causes water to leak out all the way back to your master's house. Because of my flaws, you have to do all this work, and you do not get full value for your efforts," the pot explained.

The water bearer felt sorry for the cracked pot, and in his compassion, he said, "As we return to the master's house, I want you to notice the beautiful flowers along the path." Indeed, as they went up the hill, the cracked pot took notice of the sun warming the beautiful wild flowers on the side of the path, and this cheered it a little.

But, at the end of the trail, it still felt bad because it had still leaked half of its load, and so again the pot apologized to the bearer for its failure. The bearer said to the pot: "Did you notice that there were flowers only on your side of the path, but not on the other pot's side? That is because I have always known about your flaw, and I took advantage of it. I planted flower seeds on your side of the path, and every day while we walk back from the stream, you have watered them. For two years I have been able to pick those beautiful flowers to decorate my master's table. Without you being just the way you are, he would not have this beauty to grace his house."

Each of us has our own unique flaws. We are all cracked pots. Don't be ashamed of your flaws. Acknowledge them, and you too can be the cause of beauty. Please know that in our weakness we find our strength.

幸福的人

【埃及】纳吉布·马赫福兹

他一早醒来发觉自己很幸福，是的，除了"幸福"，他再也找不着更能准确地描述自己此时心境的词汇了。今天与平日里的感觉显然不同，往日里，因为前一天在报社开夜车，所以早晨醒来总是迷迷糊糊的。然后，他还要给自己打气，才有勇气去面对生活的一切艰难和种种烦心事。

他津津有味地吃着早饭，同时对伺候他的贝希尔大叔粲然一笑："告诉我，贝希尔'大叔'，我是一个幸福的人吗？"可怜的贝希尔大叔大吃一惊，因为，虽然主人平日里待他不错，可跟他说话也只是朝着他所在的方向发号施令而已。

"承蒙真主的高贵和恩赐，您是幸福的人。"

"你的意思是说我应该感到很幸福，因为不论是谁，如果拥有我现在这样的工作，拥有我这样的健康，住在我这样的房子里，都理所当然是幸福的。不过，你以为我真的幸福吗？"

仆人贝希尔答道："您工作太辛苦啦，先生。"在他一而再再而三地追问下，他又补充道："您人爱动气啦，跟邻居争论也太爱较真……"

主人朗声大笑，打断了仆人的话，"你呢，你就没有发愁的事吗？"

"当然有，人人都有的。"

"你是说幸福是位永远也请不到的客人啰？"

"这符合生活的规律……"

仆人怎么能设想出他所感受到的令人难以置信的幸福呢？走在报馆大楼的会议厅里，他看到自己最大的政敌此时正坐在对面翻看杂志。对方显然也看见了他，却低着头盯着杂志，是为了眼不见心不烦吧。在以往的一些会议上，他们曾面红耳赤地争吵到白热化的程度，两个人唇枪舌剑，出语尖刻，有一次还动了拳头。一个星期之前，对方在工会选举中获胜，他却败下阵来，当时他感觉犹如毒箭、利箭穿身，眼前的世界也随之黯淡下来。而此刻他正向敌人的座位走去，怀揣着一颗无忧无虑的心和一脸的宽恕接纳，好像不是接近宿敌，而是去跟故交叙旧似的。他毫无芥蒂地开了口："早上好！"

敌人惊愕地抬起头，半晌没反应过来，最后才简短地应了一声，好像不敢相信自己的眼睛和自己的耳朵似的。

他挨着敌人坐下来："今天的天气真不错哈……"

"还可以……"对方心存戒备。

"是个让人内心充满幸福的好天气。"

对方靠近了些，小心翼翼地低声说道："看到你这么幸福，我很高兴……"

"惊人的幸福……"他哈哈大笑。

对方用迟疑的口气说："但愿我不会在政务会上扫了你的兴……"

"哪儿的话，我观点大家都知道，可我并不在意其他委员采用你的意见哦，这不会毁了我的幸福。"

"你一夜之间改变了许多。"对方笑吟吟地说。

"事实上是因为我幸福，惊人的幸福。"

对方仔细地审视着他的脸："是不是你的宝贝儿子改变了主意，不留在加拿大了?！"

"绝对不是，绝对不是，我的朋友，"他回答，笑声更爽朗了，"他依然坚持他的决定……"

"可这曾经是你情绪低落的主要原因啊……"

"没错儿，我以前是曾经苦苦哀求过他可怜我年老孤独，还劝他回来报效祖国。其实，他在哪里感觉幸福，就让他在哪里生活好啦。我在这里也很幸福——就像你所看到的，惊人的幸福。"

对方看到他坦露心迹，感到心里热乎乎的："说实话，我一直把你想象成一个脾气暴烈的人，这种性格给你自己和别人都带来了不少麻烦。"

"真的?"

"你不懂得休战，没有折中的概念，凶狠好斗，好像任何问题都生死攸关似的！"

"说得对。"

他以坦荡的心轻松地接受了这一批评。

几天以后，他来到一家内科医生的诊所，对医生讲述了这几天的情况。不料，他的话还没说完，医生就用手势打断了他，"一种无法抗拒的、不可思议的、使人沉迷的幸福感?"医生平静地问。

他目瞪口呆地盯着医生，正要说点什么时，医生又开了口："这种幸福感已经使你厌倦工作，放弃了朋友，憎恶睡眠……"

"你真神！"他失声大叫。

"每次遭遇不幸时，你用哈哈大笑来化解?"精神病医生问。

"先生……你是隐形人吧?"

"不是！"医生笑眯眯地回答，"只因为我每星期接待的患者中，至少有一个跟你一样！"

"你有没有发现这些人这里有些错乱？"他急切地问，同时用手指了指自己的头。

"绝对不是，"医生胸有成竹地回答，"我敢肯定他们的智力完全正常……"

医生沉吟片刻，"我们一周进行两次治疗怎么样？"

"好的。"他顺从地答应了。

"不要感到奇怪，也不要难过。"

感到奇怪？难过？他微微笑着，接着，嘴越咧越大，迸发出一声大笑，他想自控，但这一抵抗立刻土崩瓦解了，竟哈哈大笑不止。

The Happy Man

By Naguib Mahfouz

He woke up in the morning and discovered that he was happy. He could not think of any word which described his state of mind more accurately and precisely than "happy". This was distinctly peculiar when compared with the state he was usually in when he woke up. He would be half-asleep from being so late at the newspaper office. Then he would get up, whetting his determination to face up to all inconveniences and withstand all difficulties.

He ate his breakfast with a relish. He gave "Uncle" Bashir, who was waiting on him, such a beaming smile that the poor man felt rather alarmed and taken aback. Usually he would only look in his direction to give orders or ask questions, although, on most occasions, he treated him fairly well. "Tell me, 'Uncle' Bashir," he asked the servant, "am I a happy man?"

"Through God's grace and favor, you are happy," the servant replied.

"You mean, I should be happy. Anyone with my job, living in my house, and enjoying my health, should be happy. That's what you want to say. But do you think I'm really happy？"

The servant replied, "You work too hard, Sir." after yet more insistence, "You get angry a lot," he said, "and have fierce arguments with your neighbor…"

He interrupted him by laughing loudly. "What about you？" he asked. "Don't you have any worries？"

"Of course, no man can be free of worry."

"You mean that complete happiness is an impossible quest？"

"That applies to life in general…"

How could he have dreamed up this incredible happiness? In the meeting hall of the newspaper building, he spotted his main rival in this world sitting down thumbing through a magazine. The man heard his footsteps but did not look up from the magazine. He had undoubtedly noticed him in some way and was therefore pretending to ignore him so as to keep his own peace of mind. At some meetings, they would argue so violently with each other that sparks began to fly and they would exchange bitter words. One stage more, and they would come to blows. A week ago, his rival had won in the union elections, and he got lost. He had felt pierced by a sharp, poisoned arrow, and the world had darkened before his eyes. Now here he was approaching his rival's seat; He approached him with a pure and carefree heart, his face showed an expression full of tolerance and forgiveness. It was as though he were approaching some other man toward whom he had never had any feelings of enmity, or perhaps he might be renewing a friendship again. "Good morning!" he said without feeling any compunction.

The man looked up in amazement. He was silent for a few moments until he recovered, and then returned the greeting curtly. It was as though he did not believe his eyes and ears.

He sat down alongside the man. "Marvelous weather today..." he said.

"Okay..." the other replied guardedly.

"Weather to fill your heart with happiness."

His rival looked at him closely and cautiously. "I'm glad that you're so happy..." he muttered.

"Inconceivably happy..." he replied with a laugh.

"I hope," the man continued in a rather hesitant tone of voice, "that I shan't spoil your happiness at the meeting of the administrative council..."

"Not at all. My views are well-known, but I don't mind if the members adopt your point of view. That won't spoil my happiness!"

"You've changed a great deal overnight," the man said with a smile.

"The fact is that I'm happy, inconceivably happy."

The man examined his face carefully. "I bet your dear son has changed his mind about staying in Canada?!" he asked.

"Never, never, my friend," he replied, laughing loudly. "He is still sticking to his decision…"

"But that was the principal reason for your being so sad…"

"Quite true. I've often begged him to come back out of pity for me in my loneliness and to serve his country. Let him live where he'll be happy. I'm quite happy—as you can see, inconceivably happy…"

The other man warmed to his display of affection. "The truth is," he said, "that I always picture you as someone with a fierce and violent temperament which causes him a good deal of trouble and leads him to trouble other people."

"Really?"

"You don't know how to make a truce; you've no concept of intermediate solutions. You fight bitterly, as though any problem is a matter of life and death!"

"Yes, that's true."

He accepted the criticism without any difficulty and with an open heart.

A few days later he came into a clinic of his friend, the specialist in internal medicine. He began to tell the doctor his story, but the latter stopped him with a gesture of his hand. "An overwhelming, incredible, debilitating happiness?" he asked quietly.

He stared at him in amazement and was on the point of saying something, but the doctor spoke first. "A happiness which has made you stop working," he asked, "abandon your friends, and detest going to sleep..."

"You're a miracle！" he shouted.

"Every time you get involved in some misfortune," the psychiatrist continued quietly, "you dissolve into laughter..."

"Sir... are you familiar with the invisible？"

"No！" he said with a smile, "nothing like that. But I get a similar case in my clinic at least once a week！"

"Have you noticed any of them to be deranged in..." he asked anxiously, pointing to his head.

"Absolutely not," the doctor replied convincingly. "I assure you that they're all intelligent tin every sense of the word..."

The doctor thought for a moment. "We should have two sessions a week, I think？" he said.

"Very well..." he replied in resignation.

"There's no sense in getting alarmed or feeling sad..."

Alarmed, sad? He smiled, and his smile kept on getting broader, and before long, he was dissolving into laughter. He was determined to control himself, but this resistance collapsed completely. He started guffawing loudly...

幸福在哪里

【英】克里斯滕·戈德西

从前，有个女人生活在乡下的一个偏远荒僻的小山村。村里除了马匹、鲜花和人之外，什么都没有。她小的时候，生活就在等待中度过，长大以后才离开家乡去看外面的世界。她心里很清楚，生活中除了马匹、鲜花和人之外，还有其他内容。多年以来，她一分一分地攒钱，终于攒够了到异国他乡的旅费。

村民们都聚拢起来与她道别。村里的长者对她致以良好的祝愿，要她平安健康地归来。

女人来到第一个异国他乡，遇到了大量以前从来没有见过的奇妙东西。有那么多珍禽异兽、美味珍馐，那么多的声音和面孔让她应接不暇，不知所措。她在那块土地上漫无目的地走着，努力去理解和牢记许多东西。

有一天，她看到一个马厩。马厩的主人正在院子里在照料马，女人从来没有见过这么精良的马。

"下午好。"女人打了个招呼。

"下午好。"马厩的主人回答。

"你的马非常可爱呢。"女人赞叹道。

"谢谢你。你是外地人吧？"

"是啊。"

"你的家乡有精良的马吗？"

"在没见到你的马之前，我一直以为我们家乡的马是最精良的，现在我认为你的马更精良。"

"饲养出精良的马可不是一件容易的事，"马厩的主人解释说，"过来，我领你看看，再解释一下我说的话。"

马厩的主人带着女人在院子里四处走，给她看他饲养的各种各样的马。这么多马，外形、毛色各异，大小不同，女人确实吃惊不小。

"我以前根本不知道马的种类会有这么多。"

"它们不只是外表不同，内在也不同。你要学会怎么相马，"马厩的主人说，"它们的精神在眼睛里。"

女人仔细研究了许多马的眼睛，发现马的内在的确像外在一样各不相同。她从马厩的主人那里学到了更多关于马的知识，所以临别的时候向他道谢。

她回到家乡的小村庄以后，首先留意的就是马。以前，她一直以为家乡的马是好马，由于天天看得见，司空见惯，所以从来也没有更多地关注这些马。现在，她仔细地研究这些马的眼睛，这些都是跟她一起长大的马，这些马也都能认出她来，她第一次看到了这些马的精神，她笑了。

村民围拢在她的周围，好奇地看着她。村长问她在旅途中都学到了什么。

她告诉他们："我学会了怎么相马。"

村民们面面相觑，纷纷耸肩，不以为然。

"我们村的马非常精良。"女人说道。

　　她在马厩找了份工作，负责训练和照料马，为了下次出国旅行一分钱一分钱地攒着。

　　她攒够了钱以后，村民们都聚集到一起跟她道别，村里的长者对她致以良好的祝愿，要她平安健康地归来。

　　女人到了第二个异国他乡，第二次遇到了大量以前从来没有见过的东西。仍有那么多珍禽异兽、美味珍馐，那么多的声音和面孔，让她应接不暇，不知所措，不过她比第一次淡定了些。她在那块土地上漫无目的地走着，努力去理解和牢记许多东西。

　　有一天，她看到一个她从未见过的最甜美的庭院，满庭馨郁芬芳的花朵。

　　"下午好。"女人打了个招呼。

　　"下午好。"园丁回答。

　　"那些鲜花真是甜美芬芳呢。"

　　"谢谢你，"园丁回答，"你从哪里来？"

　　"我从异国他乡的一个遥远的小山村来。"

　　"你们村里有花吗？"

　　"有啊，不过没有你的花香浓郁。"

　　"吐露芬芳的不是花，"园丁倚在花锄上回答，"香不香在于你闻花的方式。过来。"

　　女人穿过花园，看到了大量的鲜花，她都不敢相信是真花。

　　"你要张开嘴这样闻才行。"说着，园丁朝花床俯下身来，张开嘴，深深地吸了一口气。女人也学着他的样子闻，于是闻到了她能想象到的最甜美的花香。她走遍了花园，闻遍了所有的鲜花，发现满庭芬芳，争奇斗艳，香味各异，她惊诧不已，流连忘返。

　　她从园丁那里学到了许多知识，所以临别的时候向他道谢。

当她回到了家乡，那个偏远荒僻的乡下，那个小村庄，她最先留意的就是鲜花。她以前一直以为这些鲜花气味芬芳，却从来没有真正更多地留意过，是因为每天都能闻到，已经司空见惯了。此时，她俯下身来，张开嘴，深深地吸了一口气，觉得鲜花比她记忆中的要香，不仅如此，由于香味是熟悉的，所以感觉胜过了那个园丁家的满庭芬芳。

村民聚拢在她的周围，村里的长者问她在异国他乡都学到了什么。

"我学会了怎么闻花。"她回答。

村民们面面相觑，纷纷耸肩，不以为然。

"我们村的鲜花芬芳怡人，非常好。"

她在花园找了份工作，种花除草，一分一分地攒着钱，终于攒够了下一次到异国他乡的旅费。

当她对村民们说，她又要离开，村里人都很伤感，他们不抱希望了，他们说，她见过那么多世面，做过那么多工作，所以她绝对不会成为他们中的一员，绝对不会在这样一个小村庄里安居乐业，传宗接代。所有的村民都聚拢到她周围，向她道别。

村里的长者对她致以良好的祝愿，要她平安健康地归来。

女人到了第三个异国他乡，既看到了许多没有见过的新鲜东西，也看到了许多以前见过的东西。她喜欢体验新的动物、食物、声音和面庞，却发现这些与自己见过的相差无几。她在那块土地上漫无目的地走着，发现自己理解和牢记了许多东西。

有一天，她坐在人行道上休息。她累了，就在那里坐了好几个小时，看着来往的行人。一个老头在她身旁坐了下来，问道："你不是本地人吧？"

"不是，"女人回答，"我从远方国度的一个小村庄来。"

"那你到这里来干什么呢？"

老人的眼睛是湿润和和善的。

"我……"女人犹豫起来，"我也不知道。"

老人幽幽长叹。

"你觉得这些拥有好东西的人幸福吗？"她问道。

"拥有好东西的人幸福？不对，不对，"老人说道，"只有人才能让人幸福。你需要知道怎么去爱别人就够了。人不是东西；人会思考，人有感觉。你要告诉别人你爱他们，你要把爱展示给他们看。你要说金玉良言，要有真情实感。要欣赏人们原本的样子，不要期待他们去做他们做不到的事情，也不要期待得到他们所不能给予的东西。然而，最重要的是，你要让他们爱上你。人是古怪的动物，人与人之间，在诸多方面会千差万别。不过，我们都有一个共同点，那就是，我们都需要爱。"老人凝视着街对面，陷入了沉思。"你只要了解这些就够啦。"

女人点了点头。

"你教给了我许多东西，老爷子，谢谢你。"

"找爱你的人去吧。"他说道。

女人回到了家乡的小村庄，所有的村民都聚拢过来欢迎她。他们看着她，对她微笑，她平生第一次注意到他们的面庞是那样友善。由于往日里司空见惯了，其实，她以前从来没有真正注意过他们。现在，她看出他们都是那么爱她。

长者问她学到了什么。

"我学会了去爱人。"她回答，眼里含着幸福的泪水。

村民们都纷纷点头称是。

"这里有非常良善的人。"

长者向女人走了过去，伸开双臂拥着她。

"你想看的东西都看了吗？"

女人点了点头。她深深地吸了一口气，卷起袖子来准备大干一场。她得找个人帮她造人，开枝散叶了。

她有很多人生感悟要传授给后人。

Lessons of the Foreign Land

By Kristen Ghodsee

There was once a woman who lived in a small village in the smallest enclave of the countryside. There was nothing in this village except horses and flowers and people. All of her life she had waited until she was old enough to leave the village and see the world. She knew in her heart there was more to life than horses and flowers and people. For many years she saved money, coin by coin, until she had enough to make her first journey to a foreign land.

All of the villagers gathered to bid her farewell. The village elder gave her his good wishes and asked that she return to the village safely and in good health.

The woman went to the first foreign land and was met with a circus of wonderful things she had never seen before. There were so many new and unusual animals and foods and sounds and faces that the woman was overwhelmed. She wandered through the land and tried to understand and remember many things.

One day she came upon a stable. The stable master was in the yard grooming his horses. They were the finest horses the woman had ever seen.

"Good afternoon, " the woman said.

"Good afternoon, " said the stable master.

"You have very lovely horses, " said the woman.

"Thank you. You are a stranger here, aren't you? "

"Yes."

"Do they have fine horses where you come from? "

"I had always thought that our horses were the finest horses in the world. But now that I see yours, I think that yours are finer."

"No easy task to breed fine horses," said the stable master. "Come here and I'll show you what I mean."

The stable master took the woman around his grounds and showed her the different kinds of horses he kept. There were so many different shapes and colors and sizes of horse that the woman was truly amazed.

"I never knew there were so many kinds of horse."

"That's only the outside. They are all different on the inside, too. You have to know how to look at a horse, " said the stable master. "The spirit of them is in the eyes."

The woman looked into the eyes of many horses and saw that they were truly as varied on the inside as on the outside. She learned much about horses from the stable master and thanked him when she left.

When she returned to her village, the first thing she noticed was the horses. She had always thought they were fine horses. But the woman had never paid much attention to them before because she had seen them every day of her life. She looked into their eyes. These were the horses she had grown up with, and they recognized her. The woman saw their spirits for the first time. She smiled.

The villagers gathered around her, watching her curiously. The village elder asked her what she had learned on her travels.

She told them, "I learned how to look at horses."

The villagers glanced at each other, shrugging their shoulders.

"We have very fine horses in this village," the woman said.

She took a job in the stables, training and grooming the horses. She saved her money, coin by coin, for her next journey abroad.

When she had saved enough all of the villagers gathered to bid her farewell. The village elder gave her his good wishes and asked that she return to the village safely and in good health.

The woman went to the second foreign land and was met with another circus of wonderful things she had never seen before. There were so many new and unusual animals and foods and sounds and faces that she was still overwhelmed, but less so than the first time. She wandered through the land and tried to understand and remember many things.

One day she came upon a garden full of sweetest smelling flowers she had ever smelled.

"Good afternoon," said the woman.

"Good afternoon," said the gardener.

"Those are sweet smelling flowers."

"Thank you," said the gardener, "Where are you from?"

"I'm from a small village, in a distant country."

"Do you have flowers in your village?"

"Yes, but your flowers smell far sweeter."

"It's not the flowers that smell sweet," said the gardener, leaning on his hoe. "It's how you smell them. Come here."

The woman walked through the garden and saw so many flowers she could not believe they were all real.

"You have to smell them with your mouth open, like this." The gardener leaned over the flower beds with his mouth open and took a deep breath. The woman did the same and inhaled the most beautiful scent she could imagine. She walked throughout the garden smelling all the flowers and was lost in amazement at the differences in their aromas, each splendid in its own way.

She learned much from the gardener and thanked her when she left.

When she returned to her little village in its little enclave in the countryside, the first thing she noticed was the flowers. She had always thought that they were nice-smelling flowers, but had never really paid much attention to them because she had smelled them every day of her life. She leaned over them and took a deep breath with her mouth open. The flowers smelled better than she ever remembered. And because the scent was a familiar one, it was better than all the flowers in the gardener's garden.

The villagers gathered and the village elder asked her what she had learned while she was gone.

"I learned how to smell flowers." she said.

The villagers looked at each other and shrugged.

"We have very good flowers in this village."

She began to work in the gardens, planting flowers and pulling weeds, saving her money, coin by coin, until she had enough to go on her next journey.

The villagers were sad when she told them she was leaving again. They were losing hope. She would never be one of them, they said. She could never settle down and have children and enjoy her life in such a small village when she had seen and done so much. All the villagers gathered to bid her farewell.

The village elder gave her his good wishes and asked that she return to the village safely and in good health.

The woman went to the third foreign land and saw many things she had seen before, although there were still many new things. She enjoyed experiencing the new animals and foods and sounds and faces, but found that they were not that much different than the ones she had seen before. She wandered through the land and found she understood and remembered many things.

One day she sat down on a sidewalk to rest. She was tired and sat for many hours watching the people walk past. An old man sat beside her. "You're not from here, are you? "

"No, " said the woman, "I come from a small village, far away in another country."

"What are you doing here then? "

The old man's eyes were watery and kind.

"I'm…" The woman hesitated, "I don't know."

The old man sighed.

"Do you think all these people are happy with the wonderful things they have? " She asked.

"People happy with things? No, no, " the old man said. "Only people make people happy. You just have to know how to love people. People aren't things; people think, they feel. You have to tell them you love them. You have to show them. You have to say nice things. You have to mean them. You have to appreciate people for what they are. You can't expect more than they can do or give. But most important, you have to let them love you. People are funny creatures, and everyone is different from everybody else in thousands of different ways. But we all have one thing in common. We all need love." The old man stared across the street, lost in thought for a moment. "That's all you need to know."

The woman nodded her head.

"I have learned much from you, old man. Thank you."

"Find the people that love you, " he said.

When the woman returned to her village, all of the villagers gathered to welcome her. They looked at her and smiled at her and for the first time she noticed how friendly and kind their faces were. Since she had seen them every day of her life, she had never truly noticed them before. She saw that they all loved her well.

The village elder asked her what she had learned.

"I learned to love people," she said with tears of happiness in her eyes.

The villagers nodded.

"There are very good people here."

The village elder went to the woman and put his arms around her.

"Have you seen all the things you wanted to see?"

The woman nodded. She took a deep breath and rolled up her sleeves. She would have to find somebody to help her make more people.

She would have many things to teach them.

实话实说

【印度】R.K. 卡拉扬

塞卡尔反思着：实话，就像太阳一样，没有谁在直视它时能不眨眼不眼花缭乱的。他认识到：人们之间的关系的本质靠软化了的实话来维系，从而避免让对方感到震惊。他把今天定为独一无二的日子——今天，不论发生什么，他要完完全全地接受实话，并且对别人实话实说。一生中能有这样的一天，也不枉在世上走一遭。他对谁也没有说起这个实验，在他看来，即将开始的今天充满了各种各样的可能。

太太给他端来了早餐，第一个测试就此开始。看着太太自诩为大师级的烹饪珍品，他表现得不够踊跃，于是她问："咦，不好吃吗？"若在平日，顾及她的感情，他一定会说："我觉得很饱，就是这样。"可今天他说："这玩意儿可真难吃，我根本无法下咽。" 看到她畏畏缩缩的样子，他心中暗想：没办法，实话就像太阳。

他的第二个测试发生在公共场合。一个同事走过来说："某某死了，你听说了吗？很遗憾吧？"塞卡尔回答道："不遗憾。"那个同事又开了口："他是那么好的一个人……"塞卡尔打断了他的话："远非如此，他给我的印象就是个自私自利、吝啬小气的小人。"

临下班时，塞卡尔正在教地理课的时候，接到校长写来的条子，上面写着："请在回家前来找我。"塞卡尔自言自语：一定是关于那些可怕试卷的事，一百多份男孩子龙飞凤舞的卷子啊，我已拖了好几个星期，这段时间一直觉得头上像悬着一把利剑似的。

下课铃声响了，男孩子们冲出了教室。

塞卡尔在校长室外面停下了脚步，把外套的扣子扣好，扣子问题是校长常常训导的另一个话题。

他走进校长室，彬彬有礼地说："你好，先生。"

校长抬起头来异常友好地看着他，问："今晚有空吗？"

塞卡尔答道："只有一件事，就是在家的时候答应了孩子们去郊游。"

"嗯，那你可以改天再去，现在跟我回家吧。"

"哦，好的，先生，当然……"接着，他又怯生生地问道，"哦……有什么特别的事吗，先生？"

"有啊，"校长答道，同时自顾自地微笑着，"你不知道我在音乐方面的缺憾吧？"

"哦，知道……先生。"

"我一直在偷偷地练习，而现在，也就是今天晚上，我要你到我家听一听，我还雇了鼓手和小提琴手给我伴奏，这是我第一次盛装演唱，我想征求你的意见，我知道你的看法一定很有价值。"

塞卡尔的音乐品位赫赫有名，在本市以最著名的毒舌批评家著称，他却没料到这份爱好会把他带入第三个测试。他们朝校长家走去，校长边走边可怜巴巴地说："你很惊讶是不是？我闭门苦练，在这上面花了一大笔钱。上帝没有赐给我孩子，但至少不要剥夺音乐的慰藉。"校长不住嘴地絮叨音乐的话题：那天怎样因为无聊才开始学音乐，老师一开始怎样嘲笑他，而后又怎样给予他希望，他生活中的最大愿望就是怎样在音乐中陶醉忘我，等等。

到了校长家，校长请塞卡尔在一块红色丝质地毯上落座，在他的面前摆了几碟精美的食品，他小题大做，异常殷勤地前忙后，好像塞卡尔是他的乘龙快婿。他甚至说："唔，你一定要放松心情来听，不要为那些考卷发愁。"他半开玩笑地又加了一句，"我会给你一周时间的。"

"十天行吗，先生？"塞卡尔请求道。

"好的，批准啦。"校长慨然应允。塞卡尔现在真是倍感轻松，他可以以每天十份的速度出击，摆脱这桩苦差了。

校长燃起了香，他解释说："为了营造合适的气氛。"鼓手和小提琴手已经在一块仰光垫上就座正等着他，校长像音乐会上的职业歌手一样坐到了鼓手和小提琴手中间，他清了清嗓子，唱了句印度即兴歌曲，而后停下来问道："挺不错的传统民歌，不是吗？"塞卡尔佯装没听见问话。校长又完整地唱了支塞亚甘拉贾创作的歌，接着又唱了两首。校长演唱的过程中，塞卡尔心里暗暗品评：他呱呱的声音像一打青蛙在鸣叫，他的吼声像头水牛，此时他的声音又像暴风雨中没拉紧的百叶窗了。

香快要燃尽了，两个小时过去了，塞卡尔的太阳穴在这种刺激耳膜强烈的混合音响作用下突突直跳，人也进入了半麻木状态。校长的嗓子也快哑了。终于，校长停了下来，问："还接着唱吗？"塞卡尔答道："先生，这就可以啦。"塞卡尔发现校长看起来很是震惊，已经汗流满面了，心头情不自禁地涌起了对他深切的怜悯，哪个法官在宣判之前所感受到的痛苦和无奈都不如他现在所感受到的深。他还注意到校长太太从厨房探头探脑，神情热切充满希冀。鼓手和小提琴手如释重负，神态轻松。校长摘下眼镜，拭了拭眉上的汗，问："请说说您的看法吧。"

"不好，先生……"塞卡尔吞吞吐吐地答。

"哦……接着上课会有用吗？"

"一堂也不用上啦，先生……"塞卡尔的声音在颤抖，他意识到：

实话实说比接受实话还难。

回到家，妻子沉着脸给他端上饭菜，他知道她还在为早晨的话生气。今天的两大灾难，塞卡尔自言自语：倘若测试一周，恐怕会众叛亲离。

翌日，塞卡尔在教室接到校长的电话，他忐忑不安地上了楼。

校长说："你的建议很有用，我已经把音乐老师辞退了，这么长时间，谁也不肯对我说实话。都这么个岁数了，何苦老不正经？谢谢你。顺便问一句，那些考卷判得怎么样啦？"

"您给了我十天时间。"

"哦，我重新考虑了一下，明天非要不可！"一天判一百份卷子！这意味着要熬个通宵！"给我两天时间吧，先生……"

"不行，我明天就要。还有，记着：每份考卷都要判仔细！"

"是，先生。"塞卡尔回答，心想，通宵夜战判百份考卷，对于奢侈的实话实说试验来说代价还不算大。

Like the Sun

By R.K. Narayan

Truth, Sekhar reflected, is like the sun. I suppose no human being can ever look it straight in the face without blinking or being dazed. He realized that, morning till night, the essence of human relationships consisted in tempering truth so that it might not shock. This day he set apart as unique day—at least one day in a year we must give and take absolute Truth whatever may happen. Otherwise life is not worth living. The day ahead seemed to him full of possibilities. He told no one of his experiment.

The very first test came while his wife served him his morning meal. He showed hesitation, which she had thought was her culinary masterpiece. She asked, "Why, isn't it good?" At other times he would have said, considering her feelings in the matter, "I feel full-up, that's all." But today he said, "It isn't good. I'm unable to swallow it." He saw her wince and said to himself, "Can't be helped. Truth is like the sun."

His next trial was in the common room when one of his colleagues came up and said, "Did you hear of the death of so and so? Don't you think it a pity?" "No," Sekhar answered. "He was such a fine man..." the other began. But Sekhar cut him short with: "Far from it. He always struck me as a mean and selfish brute."

During the last period when he was teaching geography, Sekhar received a note from the headmaster: "Please see me before you go home." Sekhar said to himself: It must be about these horrible test papers. A hundred papers in the boys'scrawls; he had shirked this work for weeks, feeling all the time as if a sword were hanging over his head.

The bell rang and the boys burst out of the class.

Sekhar paused for a moment outside the headmaster's room to button up his coat; that was another subject the headmaster always sermonized about.

He stepped in with a very polite "Good evening, sir."

The headmaster looked up at him in a very friendly manner and asked, "Are you free this evening?"

Sekhar replied, "Just some outing which I have promised the children at home..."

"Well, you can take them out another day. Come home with me now."

"Oh... yes, sir, certainly..." And then he added timidly, "Anything special, sir?"

"Yes," replied the headmaster, smiling to himself... "You

didn't know my weakness for music?"

"Oh, yes, sir..."

"I've been learning and practicing secretly, and now I want you to hear me this evening. I've engaged a drummer and a violinist to accompany me—this is the first time I'm doing it full-dress and I want your opinion. I know it will be valuable."

Sekhar's taste in music was well known. He was one of the most dreaded music critics in the town. But he never anticipated his musical inclinations would lead him to this trail... "Rather a surprise for you isn't it?" asked the headmaster. "I've spent a fortune on it behind doors..." They started for the headmaster's house. "God hasn't given me a child, but at least let him not deny me of the consolation of music," the headmaster said, pathetically, as they walked. He incessantly chattered about how music: how he began one day out of sheer boredom; how his teacher at first laughed at him, and then gave him hope; how his ambition in life was to forget himself in music.

At home the headmaster proved very ingratiating. He sat Sekhar on a red silk carpet, set before him several dishes of delicacies, and fussed over him as if he were a son-in-law of the house. He even said,

"Well, you must listen with a free mind. Don't worry about these test papers." He added humorously, "I will give you a week's time."

"Make it ten days, sir," Sekhar pleaded.

"All right, granted," the headmaster said generously. Sekhar felt really relieved now—he would attack them at the rate of ten a day and get rid of the nuisance.

The headmaster lighted incense sticks. "Just to create the right atmosphere." he explained. A drummer and a violinist, already seated on a Rangoon mat, were waiting for him. The headmaster sat down between them like a professional at a concert, cleared his throat, and began an alapana, and paused to ask, "Isn't it good Kalyani?" Sekhar pretended not to have heard the question. The headmaster went on to sing a full song composed by Thyagaraja and followed it by two more. All the time the headmaster was singing, Sekhar went on commenting within himself. He croaks like a dozen frogs. He is bellowing like a buffalo. Now he sounds like loose window shutters in a storm.

The incense sticks burnt low. Sekhar's head throbbed with the medley of sounds that had assailed his ear-drums for a couple of hours now. He felt half stupefied. The headmaster had gone nearly hoarse, when he paused to ask, "Shall I go on?" Sekhar replied, "Please don't, sir, I think this will do…" The headmaster looked stunned. His face was beaded with perspiration. Sekhar felt the greatest pity for him. But he felt he could not help it. No judge delivering a sentence felt more pained and helpless. Sekhar noticed that the headmaster's wife peeped in from the kitchen, with eager curiosity. The drummer and the violinist put away their burdens with an air of relief. The headmaster removed his spectacles, mopped his brow, and asked, "Now, come out with your opinion."

"No, sir…" Sekhar replied.

"Oh! …Is there any use continuing my lessons? "

"Absolutely none, sir…" Sekhar said with his voice trembling. Truth, he reflected, required as much strength to give as to receive.

At home his wife served him with a sullen face. He knew she was still angry with him for his remark of the morning. Two casualties for today, Sekhar said to himself. If I practice it for a week, I don't think I shall have a single friend left.

Sekhar received a call from the headmaster in his classroom next day. He went up apprehensively.

"Your suggestion was useful. I have paid off the music master. No one would tell me the truth about my music all these days. Why such antics at my age! Thank you. By the way, what about those test papers? "

"You gave me ten days, for correcting them."

"Oh, I've reconsidered it. I must positively have them here tomorrow…" A hundred papers in a day! That meant all night's sitting up! "Give me a couple of days, sir…"

"No. I must have them tomorrow morning. And remember, every paper must be thoroughly scrutinized."

"Yes, sir, " Sekhar said, feeling that sitting up all night with a hundred test papers was a small price to pay for the luxury of practicing Truth.

伤不起

【美】路易·琼斯

有一个卖布丁的商店，在圣诞季节，将许多美味的布丁食品都成排成排地陈列出来，你可以选其中最对你口味的，在决定买之前你甚至还可以品尝一下。

我一直怀疑会不会有不想真买的人利用这个便利条件只尝不买。有一天，我对一个年轻的女店员提出了这个疑惑，我了解到确实发生过这种事情。

"比如说，就有这么一个老先生，"她告诉我，"他几乎每周都来，每一种布丁都要尝一尝，可是却从来没买过，我推测他将来也绝对不会买。我记得他去年是这样，前年也是如此。嗯，他想要尝，就让他来，也欢迎他来好啦。不仅如此，我希望他可以去更多的商店，享受他那份儿，他看起来很需要很满意，我猜他们也供得起。"

她话音未落，有个上了年纪的老先生就一瘸一拐地走到柜台前，开始饶有兴致地细看那排布丁。

"唔，我跟你说的先生就是他，"年轻的女店员对我低声说，"看呐。"然后，她转向他说："先生，请品尝一下好吗？给你，用这个羹匙吧。"

老先生穿得很破旧，却很干净，他接过羹匙，开始迫不及待地挨个品尝起布丁来，只是偶尔用一块破旧的大手帕擦擦泛红的眼睛。

"这个挺不错的。"

"这个也不差，就有点腻。"

显而易见，他从头到尾都真诚地相信他最终会买一种，我可以肯定他从来没有动过欺骗店家的念头。可怜的老家伙！也许他在穷困潦倒以前，他还有钱过来选自己最喜欢的布丁的，而现在品尝布丁已经成为他残存的唯一习惯了。

在一群看起来喜气洋洋、富足幸运的圣诞购物者中间，老人瘦小的黑色身影显得很可怜，很不合时宜，我一时动了恻隐之心，向他走了过去说道：

"对不起，先生，你能帮我一个忙吗？让我给你买一份布丁，我会非常高兴。"

他像被叮了似的向后跳了一步，血涌到了他满是皱纹的脸上。

"对不起，"他说道，我没有想到他脸上的表情会有这样的自尊自贵，与他的外表那么不相符，"我不认为有认识你的荣幸，你一定是认错人了。"他迅速做出了一个决定，转身对年轻的女店员大声说："请帮我把这个包好，我要带走。"他指着其中最大和最贵的那个布丁说道。

女店员从架子上把布丁拿下来开始打包，他掏出一个破旧的黑色小皮夹，开始在柜台上数一个个先令和便士，为了维护自己的"尊严"，他在被迫买他可能买不起的东西，我多么懊悔，要是自己没说那些不得体的话有多好！弥补也太晚了，我觉得我此时能做的最大的善事就是走开。

"你可以到收银台结账。"女店员告诉他，而他好像没听懂似的，还在往她手里放硬币。此后，我再也没有听说过这个老人，也没有见过这个老人，他现在再也不能去那里品尝布丁了。

The Sampler

By Louis Jones

In a certain store where they sell puddings, a number of these delicious things are laid out in a row during the Christmas season. Here you may select the one which is most to your taste, and you are even allowed to sample them before coming to a decision.

I have often wondered whether some people, who had no intention of making a purchase, would take advantage of this privilege. One day I asked this question to the shop girl, and I learned it was indeed the case.

"Now there's one old gentleman, for instance," she told me, "he comes here almost every week and samples each one of the puddings, though he never buys anything, and I suspect he never will. I remember him from last year before that, too. Well, let him come if he wants it, and welcome to it. And what's more, I hope there are a lot more stores where he can go and get his share. He looks as if he needed it all right, and I suppose they can afford it."

She was still speaking when an elderly gentleman limped up to the counter and began looking closely at the row of puddings with great interest.

"Why, that's the very gentleman I've been telling you about," whispered the shop girl. "Just watch him now." And then turning to him: "Would you like to sample them, sir? Here's spoon for you to use."

The elderly gentleman, who was poorly but neatly dressed, accepted the spoon and began eagerly to sample one after another of the puddings, only braking off occasionally to wipe his red eyes with a large torn handkerchief.

"This is quite good."

"This is not bad either, but a little too heavy."

All the time it was quite evident that he sincerely believed that he might eventually buy one of these puddings, and I am positive that he did not for a moment feel that he was in any way cheating the store. Poor old chap! Probably he had come down in the world and this sampling was all that was left him from the time when he could afford to come and select his favorite pudding.

Amidst the crowd of happy, prosperous looking Christmas shoppers, the little black figure of the old man seemed pitiful and out of place, and in a burst of benevolence, I went up to him and said:

"Pardon me, sir, will you do me a favor? Let me purchase you one of these puddings. It would give me such pleasure."

He jumped back as if he had been stung, and the blood rushed into his wrinkled face.

"Excuse me," he said, with more dignity than I would have thought possible considering his appearance, "I do not believe I have the pleasure of knowing you. Undoubtedly you have mistaken me for someone else." And with a quick decision he turned to the shop girl and said in a loud voice, "Kindly pack me up this one here. I will take it with me." He pointed at one of the largest and most expensive of the puddings.

The girl took down the pudding from its stand and started to make a parcel of it, while he pulled out a worn little black pocketbook and began counting out shillings and pennies on to the counter. To save his "honor" he had been forced into a purchase which he could not possibly afford. How I longed for the power to unsay my tactless words! It was too late though, and I felt that the kindest thing I could do now would be walk away.

"You pay at the desk," the shop girl was telling him, but he did not seem to understand and kept trying to put the coins into her hand. And that was the last I heard of or saw of the old man. Now he can never go there to sample pudding any more.

淑　女

【南非】迪纳·帕德亚奇

　　我要给你讲的故事发生在很多年以前，当时，尼尔森·曼德拉还在罗宾岛上。事实上，那是 1980 年，我们省的医院还在实行隔离政策，不用我说，你也会明白，所有的黑人医院都是患者人满为患，医务人员匮乏。

　　我在最为繁忙的公立医院的一个小诊室里，我的服务对象通常是衣衫褴褛、身心崩溃的南非人。而那天一个穿着整齐的小伙子大踏步地昂然而入，在我的办公桌上一屁股坐了下来，俨然主人。我发现他头的一侧插着一块亮闪闪的钢片，由于多年的行医生涯，我对人体各部位——胸上、四肢上、肚子上所插的各种各样骇人的凶器——刀子、斧头等早已司空见惯，却从未见过这种钢片。

　　"是伞尖，医生。"他实打实地告诉我。

　　"你的头一定很疼吧？"我十分同情地询问。

　　"可不是嘛！头像裂了一样，可那个女人，骂个没完没了！那才是最头疼的。"至少他大脑的语言区看起来没有问题，语音清晰连贯。

　　"可要是没有了她们，我们也活不成。"我答道。我上个月终于摆脱了婚姻的束缚。我继续给他检查，尽量保持面无表情的样子。我的话并没有产生任何影响，他是个真正的老师，他还在滔滔不绝。

"是这样，有这么一个女人，我们教同一门课程，我们之间有一场争论，唔，实际上……"一丝愧疚在他脸上掠过，只停留了万分之一秒就消失无痕了，"她很漂亮，所以，迄今为止，我在她身上没少费工夫，我的朋友们一直都在笑话我，可我一点进展也没有。"他瞟了一眼门外漂亮的小护士，心照不宣地看了看我，"所以嘛，我把她一个人留在教室里，想拥吻一下，一点小小的爱的表示罢了，可她却把我推开了。"

"她已经结婚了？"我问道，想给他脆弱的自尊一个台阶下。

"结了，她还不停地说我太太是她的朋友，好像她丈夫也那么在意似的！"

他的耳膜看来很健康。

"她想给我上道德伦理课呢，还要我给学生们做榜样。女人们总是自以为是，从来不肯倾听男人们的肺腑之言。"

我满怀同情地点了点头，他继续喋喋不休，我把听诊器塞进了耳朵。我刚刚给他做完心血管和呼吸系统检查，他的话又像熔岩一样喷薄而出。我开始给他进行全面的神经系统的检查。

"当我提到她对科长的态度就非常友善时，她竟然歇斯底里地骂起人来，她用各种各样恶毒的语言咒骂我，她似乎对我们男性根本就没有尊重。这下我可忍无可忍了，于是打了她一巴掌，没什么大不了的，就是小小的一记耳光而已。"

"就像你有时打你太太似的？"我的语音和语调都恰到好处。

"就是嘛，而我也只是偶尔为之罢了，我太太理解我们男人有做这种事的心理需求，她就能接受！"他想起自己那承受能力很强的太太，摇了摇头。"可年轻的这一代女人呢，却不像我们以前那样皮实！"

"这位老师很年轻吧？"

"对，可是她属于那种不要脸的东西，她们都是一路货色：脾气大，满脑子情绪化的玩意儿，一旦受过点儿教育，就会神气活现起来！"

我点了点头表示同情："昔日那些美丽温婉的淑女都到哪里去了，莫非跟朱丽叶一起去别的牧场了？"

"就是，女人现在已经不像女人了，就挨了那么一记小小的耳光，仅此而已，就没完没了，好像我强奸了她，把她怎么样似的。"

我打定主意保持面无表情的样子，尽管这很困难。

"不知怎么着，各种妖魔鬼怪都一起登场啦，淑女已经不再是淑女了。"他又重复了一遍。

他继续说道："哼，她大喊大叫，破口大骂，说我不尊重女性，可她叫嚷的样子又有什么尊严可言！接着，她开始诅咒我的妈妈，哼，谁也不能允许任何人辱骂自己的母亲，任何人！"

我勉强保持着咧嘴的样子。

"我只一记重拳，她就倒在地板上了，我以前是班里的拳击冠军呢，我的雄风犹在。"他得意洋洋地又补充了一句。他接着吹牛："嘿，那个小贱人仰面朝天地躺在那里，看起来尊严已经荡然无存。然后，我精心测算了一下角度，在她那肥硕的屁股上狠狠地踢了一脚，我年轻时是个挺棒的棒球运动员哩。"想到这里，他快活地笑了。

我用责怪的目光看着他。我确实这么做了。

他接着说："这些小姑娘不应该招惹咱们这些膀大腰粗的大男人，她们尖刻的语言就像你们大夫用的手术刀似的。如果她们想让别人把她们当淑女对待，那她们的行为举止就应该像个淑女，当年波兰得罪了德国不就被踏踏实实地踏平了吗？"

　　我不想评论说，模仿法西斯可不是给任何人留下好印象最好方式。他看起来是一个好战的家伙，我们有不少医生曾经由于价值观与病患迥然不同而挨过打受过骂。

　　"然后我就转身离开了，我不想让人觉得我在幸灾乐祸或者别的什么。"

　　真奇怪，他还在试图为自己残忍的行为辩护。

　　"可就是在这时，那个胆小鬼抓起她的雨伞不偏不倚地刺进了我的脑袋……等我转过身去，我的头已经……"这位老师难过地摇了摇头。

　　我把他颅骨的 X 光片递给他，他非常客气地道过谢走了，身上的昂贵的科隆香水把我发霉的诊室熏得喷香。

Heavy Cerebral Metal

By Deena Padayachee

The events that I am going to tell you about occurred many years ago, when Mr. Nelson Mandela was still on Robben Island. In fact, it was in 1980 when our provincial hospitals were still segregated and it was axiomatic that all Black hospitals were overcrowded and understaffed.

As if he owned the place, a nattily dressed young man strode boldly into my medical cubicle at the busy public hospital. I usually attended to shabbily dressed South Africans, often broken both in spirit and in health. He seated himself at the wooden table which served as my work desk and greeted me. There was a piece of shiny stainless steel sticking out of the side of his head. I thought that I had seen it all during my years in *Casualty*: knives, axes, and all kinds of evil-looking weaponry in human chests, limbs, stomachs, and every part of the human anatomy. But this metallic object was one for the record books.

"That's the tip of the umbrella, doctor," he explained in a matter-of-fact voice.

"You must have a headache?" I said sympathetically.

"Oh, yes, doctor! What a splitting headache. But then again, that's women. Nag, nag, nag! They're one huge headache." At least the speech area of his brain appeared not to have been affected! His speech was not even slurred.

"But we can't survive without them." I replied. I had finally tied the knot last month. I kept my expression deadpan as I proceeded with my examination. My comment appeared to make no impression on him. He was a real teacher—he just didn't stop talking.

"You see, there's this woman. We teach on the same staff. We had an argument. Well, actually…" A shadow of guilt passed across his face for a millisecond. "She's very pretty and I've been trying my luck with her for a long time now. My friends had been teasing me, but I was getting nowhere." He glanced at the sweet little nurse outside the cubicle and gave me a knowing look. "So, when I got her alone in a classroom, I tried to embrace her and kiss her. Just a little love, that's all. But she pushed me away."

"She's married?" I asked, trying to salvage this delicate ego.

"Yes, and she keeps saying my wife is her friend. As if her husband is that careful!"

His tympanic membranes appeared healthy.

"She tried to lecture me about ethics and morals and setting an example to the kids. You know how these women go on—always thinking that they're right—never listening to what we men have to say."

I nodded sympathetically. He continued prattling away as I put the stethoscope into my ears. I had barely finished my cardiovascular and respiratory assessment when the words began issuing from his mouth again, like lava. I proceeded to perform a thorough neurological examination.

"Well, she became hysterical when I mentioned that she was very friendly with her Head of Department. She called me all kinds of names. She seems to have no respect for us Males. I just couldn't take it any more. So I slapped her. Nothing much—just a little slap."

"Like you give your wife now and again?" I enquired with just the right tone to my voice.

"Yes, but I only do that now and again. But my wife, she understands that we men need to do this sort of thing. And she can take it!" He shook his head at the memory of his resilient spouse. "But the younger generation! They're not as tough as we were."

"She's young, this teacher?"

"Yes, but she's one of the cheekiest. They are all the same; temperamental and full of mood swings. And if they have some education, they get so bucky!"

I nodded sympathetically. "Where have all the soft, sweet women gone? Gone with Juliet to other pastures?"

"Yes, women are not like women anymore. Just a teeny-weeny slap, that's all she got. But she carried on like I'd raped her or something."

I decided to keep my face expressionless, even though it was difficult.

"Anyway, all hell broke loose." He shook his head. "Ladies aren't ladies anymore," he repeated.

He continued. "Well, she screamed and shouted something awful. Said I had no respect for a lady's dignity. There wasn't anything dignified about the way she was screaming. But then she swore about my mother. Now, you can do anything you like but nobody messes with my mother. Nobody！"

Somehow, I kept from grinning.

"Anyway, I blasted her—one hell of a tight shot and she ended up on the floor. I used to be boxing champion of my class," he mentioned proudly. "I hadn't lost my touch," he boasted. "Ja, the little witch didn't look very dignified on her backside. Then for good measure, I gave her one tight kick on the side of her big bum. I was a soccer player in my time." He smiled happily at the memory.

I looked at him reproachfully; I really did.

He remonstrated. "These little girls mustn't try to provoke us big, strong guys. They like to use words the way you doctors wield scalpels. If they want us to treat them like ladies, then they must behave like ladies. I mean when Poland messed with Germany, she got beaten solid."

I decided not to comment that imitating fascists wasn't the best way to create a good impression with anybody. He looked like an aggressive fellow, and many doctors have been abused and even assaulted by patients whose values are rather different from ours.

"I walked away then; I didn't want to look like I was gloating or something."

Strange how he continued to try and rationalize his deplorable behavior.

"But then the little coward grabbed her umbrella and stabbed it right into my head...when my back was turned. *My head*!" The teacher shook his head sadly.

As I handed him the note for an X-ray of his skull, he thanked me ever so politely and disappeared, his expensive cologne sweetening the air in my musty cubicle.

跳楼姑娘

【意大利】迪诺·巴扎提

十九岁的玛尔塔站在摩天大楼的楼顶，俯瞰着黄昏中闪闪发光的城市，顿觉头晕目眩。

银色的摩天大楼在这个绝顶美丽、绝顶纯净的夜晚显得高高在上，幸运异常。站在那个高度上，女孩玛尔塔看到下面的一排排街道和一幢幢大楼在日落的长时间痉挛中扭曲，整个城市成了一个被灯光打亮的甜蜜的深渊，深渊里有男有女，有达官贵人，有毛皮衣服和小提琴，有玛瑙般亮闪闪的汽车，有通宵俱乐部的霓虹招牌，有钻石，有古老沉寂的花园，有聚会、欲望和桃色事件，而最诱惑的是魔术般的夜晚唤起的对伟大和光荣的梦想。

看到这一切，玛尔塔不由自主地越过了栏杆，让自己坠落下去，她觉得是在空中翱翔，实际上却是在坠落。由于摩天大楼高得出奇，距离地面上的街道和广场很遥远，谁知道她什么时候才能到达。而女孩在坠落。

此刻，顶楼的平台上和阳台上站满了优雅的有钱人，他们在开鸡尾酒会，他们说着傻话，谈话声比音乐声还大。玛尔塔在他们面前经过，有几个人向外看着她。

摩天大楼上这样的飞行（飞的大多数都是女孩）并不鲜见，事实上，这成了高层房客的一种饶有兴致的消遣，也是这类房价居高不下的原因。

还没有完全落下去的太阳竭力用余晖照亮玛尔塔简朴而廉价的衣衫，衣衫是在地摊上买的，落日抒情的光晕使衣衫看上去漂亮起来。

一双双勇敢的手从百万富翁的阳台上伸出来，向她伸过来殷勤地献酒、献花："小姐，喝杯酒好吗？……温柔的蝴蝶，为什么不停下来跟我们待一分钟呢？"

她笑着，飞旋着，感觉很快乐（与此同时也在坠落着）："不啦，谢谢朋友们，我不能停，我急着赶路呢。"一个身材高挑、皮肤黝黑、非常出色的小伙子伸出一只手来抓她，玛尔塔很喜欢他，可是她很快想到了自卫："你怎么敢这样，先生？"她还来得及轻轻拍打一下他的鼻子。

她满心欢喜，她自觉很迷人，很漂亮。在这个布满鲜花的平台上，在这身着白衣、忙忙碌碌的侍者中间，在这一声声充满异国情调的歌声里，曾经有过那么几分钟（也许更少）关于年轻姑娘的谈话，说她从楼顶垂直而下，有的人认为她很漂亮，有的人觉得她相貌平平，但所有的人都认为她很有趣。

与此同时，太阳跳入大海，正好，摩天大楼的大部分窗户和平台都已灯火辉煌，灯光反射的光线完全可以导引她缓缓下行。

此时，玛尔塔再也看不见屋里有无忧无虑的人了。她看到一些公司的雇员身穿黑色或者蓝色的围裙在桌前坐成长长的一排，其中有几个跟她年龄相仿或者比她大的年轻人，因为此时已经劳累了一天，所以每隔一会儿就会停下手里的活儿或者打字机抬起头来。就这样，他们也发现了她，有几个人跑到窗前，"你去哪里？干什么这么急？你是谁？"他们对她喊道，她能从他们的话里听出羡慕的意味。

"他们在下面等我呢，"她回答道，"我停不下来，原谅我吧。"夜幕已经狡猾地降临，玛尔塔开始感觉到冷了。

她向下看，只见楼的入口处有一圈黑色小汽车组成的明亮的光环（远处看上去就像蚂蚁），男男女女从车上下来，急切地冲入楼内。入口处有旗帜在飘扬。她好像能从那一大群中分辨出闪闪发光的宝石来。

他们一定是在开玛尔塔从孩提时就朝思暮想的那种大型聚会，上苍保佑她不要错过了，那里有机会、好运、爱情在等她，那才是她生活的真正开端。她会及时赶到吗？

玛尔塔忽然发现跳楼的姑娘不只她一个，摩天大楼的每个侧面都有年轻女人向下栽，她们的脸由于兴奋而绷紧，她们的手快活地挥舞着，仿佛在说：看看我们吧，我们在这里，款待我们吧，难道这世界不是我们的吗？

现在成了一场竞赛了，她只穿着件小小的寒酸外套，而别的姑娘却穿得像潇洒的高级模特一般，有些人裸露的肩膀上还紧紧地裹着奢华的貂皮围巾。玛尔塔往下跳的时候是那么信心满满，此时却浑身发抖，也许是因为冷，也许是因为害怕，害怕犯下无法挽回的错误。

此时似乎夜已深，窗户里的灯一盏盏地熄灭了，音乐声越来越小，办公室已人去楼空。那幢楼的入口处似乎变大了，可以看到建筑的细节了，依然灯火通明，但来来往往的汽车已经停止了。每隔一会儿就有一批人疲惫不堪地出门离去，接着，入口处的灯也关掉了。

玛尔塔觉得心头发紧，天哪，她没有赶上舞会。抬头望去，摩天大楼的顶尖显出冷酷的权威。天已完全黑了。

在二十八层，一个约莫四十岁左右的男人边喝咖啡边读晨报，他的太太正在收拾房间。餐具柜上的时钟显示出此时是八点四十五分。一个影子从窗口闪过。

"阿尔贝托！"他太太大叫，"你看见了吗？一个女人跳下去了。"

"什么人？"他眼皮也没抬，继续看报纸。

"一个老太婆，一个老态龙钟的老太婆，她看起来很害怕。"

"总是这样，"男人嘟嘟囔囔，"低楼层只能掉下来一些老太婆，像一百五十层以上的楼层才能看到漂亮的姑娘，那些房子要价高也不是瞎高。"

"可咱们至少有一个便利，就是可以听到落地时砰的一声。"他太太明察秋毫。

他站起来听了几分钟，而后摇了摇头："这次连那一声也没有。"他又呷了口咖啡。

The Falling Girl

By Dino Buzzati

Marta was nineteen. She looked out over the roof of the skyscraper, and seeing the city below shinning in the dusk, she was overcome with dizziness.

The skyscraper was silver, supreme and fortunate in that most beautiful and pure evening. From that height the girl saw the streets and the masses of buildings writhing in the long spasm of sunset. The city became a sweet abyss burning with lights. Within it were powerful men and women, furs and violins, cars glossy as onyx, the neon signs of nightclubs, diamonds, old silent gardens, parties, desires, affairs, and, above all, that consuming sorcery of the evening which provokes dreams of greatness and glory.

Seeing these things, Marta hopelessly leaned out over the railing and let herself go. She felt as if she was hovering in the air, but she was falling. Given the extraordinary height of the skyscraper, the streets and squares down at the bottom were very far away. Who knows how long it would take her to get there. Yet the girl was failing.

At that hour the terraces and balconies of the top floors were filled with rich and elegant people who were having cocktails and making silly conversation. Their talk muffled the music. Marta passed before them and several people looked out to watch her.

Flights of that kind （mostly by girl, in fact） were not rare in the skyscraper and they constituted an interesting diversion for the tenants; this was also the reason why the price of those apartments was very high.

The sun had not yet completely set and it did its best to illuminate Marta's simple clothing. She wore a modest, inexpensive spring dress bought off the rack. Yet the lyrical light of the sunset exalted it somewhat, making it chic.

From the millionaires'balconies, gallant hands were stretched out toward her, offering flowers and cocktails. "Miss, would you like a drink? ...Gentle butterfly , why not stop a minute with us?"

She laughed, hovering, happy （but meanwhile she was falling）: "No, thanks, friends. I can't. I'm in a hurry." A young man, tall, dark, very distinguished, extended an arm to snatch her. She liked him. And yet Marta quickly defended herself "How dare you, sir?" and she had time to give him a little tap on the nose.

She felt fascinating, stylish. On the flower-filled terraces, amid the bustle of waiters in white and the bursts of exotic songs, there was a talk for a few minutes, perhaps less, of the young woman who was passing by （from top to bottom, on a vertical course）. Some thought her pretty, others thought her so-so, everyone found her interesting.

In the meantime, however, the sun had plunged into the sea; It was a good thing that the windows and terraces of the skyscraper were almost all illuminated and the bright reflections completely gilded her as she gradually passed by.

Now Marta no longer saw just groups of carefree people inside the apartments; at times there were even some businesses where the employees, in black or blue aprons, were sitting at desks in long rows. Several of them were young as old as or older than she, and weary of the day by now, every once in a while they raised their eyes from their duties and from typewriters. In this way they too saw her, and a few ran to the windows. "Where are going? Why so fast? Who are you?" they shouted to her. One could divine something akin to envy in their words.

"They're waiting from me down there," she answered. "I can't stop. Forgive me." The night had craftily fallen and Marta started to feel cold.

Meanwhile, looking downward, she saw a bright halo of lights at the entrance of a building. Here long blacks cars were stopping (from the great distance they looked as small as ants), and men and women were getting out, anxious to go inside. She seemed to make out the sparkling of jewels in that swarm. Above the entrance flags were flying.

They were obviously giving a large party, exactly the kind

that Marta dreamed of ever since she was a child. Heaven help her if she missed it. Down there opportunity was waiting for her, fate, romance, the true inauguration of her life. Would she arrive in time?

Then she realized that along the sides of the skyscraper many other young women were plunging downward, their faces taut with the excitement of the flight, their hands cheerfully waving as if to say: look at us, here we are, entertain us, is not the world ours?

It was a contest, then. And she only had a shabby little dress while those other girls were dressed smartly like high-fashion models and some even wrapped luxurious mink stoles tightly around their bare shoulders. So self-assured when she began the leap, Marta now felt a tremor growing inside her; perhaps it was just the cold; but it may have been fear too, the fear of having made an error without remedy.

It seemed to be late at night now. The windows were darkened one after another, the echoes of music became more rare, the offices were empty. At the entrance to the building down below—which in the meantime had grown larger, and one could now distinguish all the architectural details—the lights were still burning, but the bustle of cars had stopped. Every now and then, in fact, small groups of people came out wearily drawing away. Then the lights of the entrance were also turned off.

Marta felt her heart tightening. Alas, she wouldn't reach the ball in time. Glancing upwards, she saw the pinnacle of the skyscraper in all its cruel power. It was almost completely dark.

On the twenty-eight floor a man about forty years old was having his morning coffee and reading his newspaper while his wife tidied up the room. A clock on the sideboard indicated 8:45. A shadow suddenly passed before the window.

"Alberto!" the wife shouted. "Did you see that? A woman passed by."

"Who was it?" he said without raising his eyes from the newspaper.

"An old woman," the wife answered. "A decrepit old woman. She looked frightened."

"It's always like that," the man muttered. "At these low floors only falling old women pass by. You can see beautiful girls from the hundred-and-fiftieth floor up. Those apartments don't cost so much for nothing."

"At least down here there's the advantage," observed the wife, "that you can hear the thud when they touch the ground."

"This time not even that," he said, shaking his head, after he stood listening from a few minutes. Then he had another sip of coffee.

听，蟋蟀的声音

一个人跟他的一个朋友在城里的大街上走着，时值正午，正是午饭时间，大街上人来人往，小汽车在按喇叭，出租车在拐角发出长长的尖利的声音，警报在哀鸣，城市发出的声音几乎震耳欲聋。突然，这个人对朋友说："我听到一只蟋蟀在叫。"

他的朋友反诘道："什么？你一定是疯了，这么吵你怎么可能听到蟋蟀叫呢！"

"我确实听到了，"这个人说，"我听到了一只蟋蟀的叫声。"

"太荒唐啦。"他的朋友评论道。

这个人仔细地听了一会儿，穿过马路来到一个水泥花坛前。花坛里长着一些灌木，他朝灌木里张望，果然在一些树枝下面看到了一只小蟋蟀。他的朋友被惊得目瞪口呆，"不可思议，"他的朋友惊叹，"你的耳朵一定是超人耳朵！"

"哪里是，"这个人解释道，"我的耳朵跟你的哪里有什么不同，其实一切取决于你在听什么。"

"可这怎么可能呢！"他的朋友说，"这么吵，我根本听不到蟋蟀的叫声。"

"是的，确实如此，"这个人回答，"其实，这取决于你觉得什么对于你来说是最重要的。过来，我给你演示一下。"

　　他伸手从衣服口袋里掏出几个硬币，轻轻地扔到人行道上。接下来，在人潮涌动、车水马龙，喧闹声依旧声声在耳的街上，他们注意到二十英尺以内的人个个都把头转了过来，查看人行道上叮当作响的钱是不是自己的。

　　"你明白我的意思了吗？"这个人问道。

　　"一切取决于你觉得什么对你来说是最重要的，所以，世事纷繁，分清主次很重要。"

The Cricket

A man and his friend were in a city, walking through the street. It was during the noon lunch hour and the streets were filled with people. Cars were honking their horns, taxicabs were squealing around corners, sirens were wailing, and the sounds of the city were almost deafening. Suddenly, the man said to his friend, "I hear a cricket."

His friend said, "What? You must be crazy. You couldn't possibly hear a cricket in all of this noise!"

"No, I'm sure of it," the man said, "I heard a cricket."

"That's crazy," said the friend.

The man listened carefully for a moment, and then walked across the street to a big cement planter where some shrubs were growing. He looked into the bushes, and sure enough, beneath the branches, he located a small cricket. His friend was completely amazed. "That's incredible," said his friend. "You must have super-human ears!"

"No," said the man. "My ears are no different from yours. It all depends on what you're listening for."

"But that can't be!" said the friend. "I could never hear a cricket in this noise."

"Yes, it's true," was the reply. "It depends on what is really important to you. Here, let me show you."

He reached into his pocket, pulled out a few coins, and carefully dropped them on the sidewalk. And then, with the noise of the crowded street still blaring in their ears, they noticed every head within twenty feet turn and look to see if the money that tinkled on the pavement was theirs.

"See what I mean?" asked the man.

"It all depends on what's important to you. So it's vital that you prioritize what you do."

想做真人的稻草人

【英】肯·科珀

从前，有个稻草人，他在农民史密斯家的玉米地里站了整整一个夏天，在风中挥舞着胳膊把乌鸦吓跑。他的活儿干得很不错，阻止了那些又大又黑的鸟从空中俯冲下来，在玉米长成之前就把它吃掉。

可是，他不太舒服，一点也不快乐。因为他被绑在栅栏柱上，晚上根本没法躺下，在炙热的白天，也没法进屋凉快一下。他也没法看白云在天空中轻快地飘过，因为他前额上的宽边软帽压得很低。不仅如此，他独自一人站在空旷的野外还非常孤单寂寞，除了被他赶走的鸟儿和偶尔从田里抄近路的棉尾兔，没人跟他说话。

他每天看着农民和雇工在田地里劳作，他看到他们随心所欲地在田地里大踏步地走来走去，又是播种又是收割，因为没被绑在栅栏柱上，所以不用一动不动地站着。他们有说有笑，你呼我唤，来去自由。

"我要是不做假人，做个真人有多好！"可怜的稻草人想，"我多么想自由自在！这样，我就可以摆脱这孤独的生活，到处走动，结交四方朋友了。"

就在这时，一个衣衫褴褛的流浪汉路过，坐在离稻草人不远的台阶上休息。

"哦，流浪汉先生！"稻草人喊道，"我正想见你呢！我可不可以问你一个问题？"

"随便问吧，"流浪汉回答，"不过我不一定能答得上来呢。"

"我想知道怎么才能变成一个人，"稻草人问道，"我厌倦了只做一个披着旧衣服填满稻草的人，我想变成一个友好的真人，就像在地里干活的人一样。"

"啊，"流浪汉幽幽长叹，"只有一样东西能把你变成人，那就是你口袋里得有叮当作响的钱。"

"我怎么才能搞到在口袋里叮当作响的钱呢？"

"我可给不了你这个答案，"流浪汉叹息道，"我自己还不知道怎么不工作就能搞到钱呢。"

"你是说你口袋里没钱吗？"稻草人问道。

流浪汉点了点头。

"不过你肯定是人吧。"稻草人惊奇地问。

"不，我只能算是半个人。"流浪汉羞愧地低下头，走开了。

"我怎么才能让口袋里有钱呢？"稻草人纳闷，"我工作很努力，可我还是没有钱呐。"

正在这时，农夫的儿子路过。稻草人想跟他说话，可是男孩正在低声嘟囔着什么，所以没听见稻草人的话。男孩在反反复复地问自己："我拿着学校野餐的钱，现在我要去小河里游泳，我要把钱放在谁也找不到的地方，我把钱藏到哪里好呢？"

他抬头一看，看到了稻草人，便说道："我知道了，我就把钱放在你的口袋里，亲爱的伙计！"于是他把一把钱塞进了稻草人的口袋，然后向小河边跑去，男孩子们正在那里叫他呢。

因为男孩说话声音小，稻草人根本没听到，还以为是他这么多天来在地里的劳作有了报酬。

他快乐地把口袋里的钱弄得叮当作响，"我现在变成人啦，"他喊道，觉得自己的腰杆挺直了，于是从栅栏柱上爬了下来。

他往城里走去，一路欢歌。可是等他进了城以后，谁都不跟他说话，人们从他身旁经过连"你好"都不说，他们甚至连看都不看他一眼。

稻草人非常难过，"也许是我穿的衣服不对吧，"他自言自语，"我最好换件新衣裳。"于是他进了一家商店，买了件非常好看的新套装和一顶新帽子。衣服非常合身，他穿上自己最漂亮的衣服走到街上，觉得非常得意。可是还是没有人注意他。

"恐怕钱并不能把我变成人。"稻草人幽幽长叹道。就在这时，一个小姑娘跑到街上，她径直跑到一辆汽车的前面，如果稻草人没有跟着她冲到路中央，她一定会被汽车碾过去。就在车到跟前的时候，稻草人及时救了她，把她抱到人行道上，使她转危为安。

路边目睹稻草人舍身救人的人们开始欢呼。小女孩的母亲从家里跑出来，泪流满面地对他连连称谢。

突然，稻草人一下子觉得心里暖洋洋，热乎乎的。他低头看了看自己的手和脚，发现自己的手脚不再是稻草做的，而是血肉铸成的。他听到人群在说："有了勇敢的心灵，才能成为真正的人。"

The Scarecrow Who Wanted to Be a Man

By Ken Copper

Once there was a scarecrow who stood all summer long in Farmer Smith's cornfield and waved his arms in the wind to scare away the crows. He did a good job of it, too. He kept those great, black birds from swooping down out of the sky and eating the corn before it could grow.

But he was not very comfortable and not at all happy. Since he was tied to a fence post he could never lie down at night, nor go into the house to cool himself in the heat of the day. Neither could he look up and watch the white clouds sailing through the sky, for his slouch hat was pulled too far down on his forehead. Also he was very lonely standing by himself in the wide outdoors with no one to talk to but the birds that he shooed away and occasionally a cottontail rabbit that took a short-cut through the field.

Every day he watched the farmer and his hired man working in the fields. He saw them stride to and fro as they pleased, sowing or reaping. They did not have to stand still because they were not tied to posts. They laughed and called to each other. They were free to come and go as they pleased.

"How I should like to be a real man instead of a make-believe one!" thought the poor scarecrow. "How I should like to be free! Then I should give up this lonely life and go about making friends."

Just then a tramp dressed in tattered clothes came by. He sat down to rest on a stile not far from the scarecrow.

"Oh, Mr. Vagabond!" cried the scarecrow. "You're just the one I want to see! I want to ask a question if I may."

"Ask what you like," said the tramp, "but I can't promise to give you the answer."

"I want to know what makes a man," said the scarecrow. "I'm tired of being just an old coat stuffed with straw. I want to be real and friendly and feel like the men that work in the field."

"Ah," sighed the tramp, "there is only one thing that can make you a man, and that is money jingling in your pockets."

"How do I get money to jingle in my pocket?" asked the scarecrow.

"That is something I can't tell you," signed the tramp. "I don't know how to get it myself, not without working for it."

"You mean you have no money in your own pockets?" asked the scarecrow.

The tramp shook his head.

"But surely you are a man," said the scarecrow in surprise.

"No, I am only half a man." And the tramp walked away hanging his head in shame.

"How can I get money in my pockets?" wondered the scarecrow. "I have worked hard, but still I have no money."

Just then the farmer's boy came by. The scarecrow tried to speak to him, but the boy was muttering so that he did not hear. He was saying over and over to himself, "Where shall I hide it? I have the money for our school picnic. I want to go down to the stream to swim and I want to hide the money where no one could possibly find it."

Then he looked up and seeing the scarecrow, said, "I know. I'll hide it in your pockets, old fellow!" So he thrust a handful of money into the scarecrow's pockets and ran toward the stream where the boys were calling.

The scarecrow had not heard all the boy said because he had not talked very loud, but the scarecrow thought he was being paid for his many days of labor in the field.

He jingled the money happily. "Now I am a man," he cried, and he felt his back stiffen so that he could climb down from the fence post.

Off he went toward the town singing a happy song. But when he got to town, no one would speak to him. People passed him by without so much as a "How-do-you-do." They didn't even seem to see him.

The scarecrow was very sad. "Perhaps it's my clothes," he said. "I had better get some new ones." So he went into a store and bought a new suit and a new hat. They were very becoming and he was proud to walk out onto the street all dressed up in his Sunday best. But still no one paid a bit of attention to him.

"I'm afraid money doesn't make a man," sighed the scarecrow.

Just then, a little girl ran out into the street. She ran right in front of an automobile. She would have been run over if the scarecrow had not darted out into the street after her. He picked her up just in time and carried her to the sidewalk in safety.

The people on the curb who had seen the scarecrow risk his own life to save the child, began to cheer. The mother of the little girl came running out of her house with tears streaming down her cheeks and thanked him.

All at once the scarecrow felt warm and glowing inside. He looked down at his hands and feet and saw they were no longer made of straw but were of flesh and blood. He heard the crowd say, "It takes a brave heart to make a man."

牧羊人的女儿

【美】威廉姆·萨拉杨

这是我祖母的观点，她认为是人都应该干活儿，愿上帝保佑她。刚才吃饭时，她还对我说："你必须学会一门好手艺，做一些对人有用的东西：用黏土做的陶器、用木头做的木器、用金属做的器皿或用布料做的东西。对于一个年轻人来说，不会一门值得尊敬的手艺是不对的。你会做什么？你会做一张简单的桌子、一把椅子、一个普通盘子、一块毯子、一把咖啡壶吗？你会做什么呢？"

祖母生气地看着我："我知道，人们说你是一个作家，我也认为是，你抽的烟也确实够多，满屋子都是，这让你看起来有了作家的派头。可是你必须学着做一些实实在在的东西，看得见、摸得着、用得上的东西。"

祖母曾经给我讲过一个故事：从前，有一个波斯国王，他有一个儿子，这个儿子爱上了一个牧羊人的女儿，他跑到他父亲跟前对他说："父王，我爱上了一个牧羊人的女儿，我要她成为我的妻子。"国王答道："我是国王，而你是我的儿子，我百年之后，你是要继承王位的，你怎么可以和牧羊人的女儿结婚呢？"可儿子说："父王，我什么都不知道，我只知道我爱这个女孩，想要她做我的王后。"

国王看到儿子对那个女孩的爱乃是天意，于是他说："那我就传旨给她吧。"国王唤来一个信使，说："到牧羊人的女儿家去，告诉她我儿子爱上了她，要娶她为妻。"信使走到女孩面前，对她说："国王的儿子爱上了你，要你成为他的妻子。"牧羊人的女儿却问道："国王的儿子是干什么的？"信使答道："咦，他是国王的儿子，什么活儿都不用干。"女孩却说："他必须学会干点什么活儿。"信使回来向国王转述了牧羊人女儿的话。

于是国王就对他儿子说："牧羊人的女儿希望你学会一门手艺。你现在还要她做你的妻子吗？"儿子说："要，我的初心不改，我要学着编草席。"于是，国王的儿子开始学习编各种各样五颜六色带装饰性图案的草席。三天下来，他已经能编得一手好席子。信使再次来到牧羊人的家，对牧羊人的女儿说，这些草席是国王的儿子编的。于是，女孩随着信使来到王宫，成了国王的儿子的王妃。

祖母说，一天，国王的儿子在巴格达大街闲逛时，无意间发现了一个清雅的小吃店，于是走了进去，在一张桌子前坐了下来。

祖母说，这个地方，是一个盗贼和杀人犯聚集的黑店，他们把国王的儿子抓住，扔进了一个大大的地牢里，那儿囚禁着许多城里的大人物。盗贼和杀人犯们把最胖的囚犯杀掉，用最胖的人的肉喂最瘦的囚犯，从中取乐。国王的儿子是囚犯中最瘦的，而且没人知道他是波斯国王的儿子，这才保全了性命，于是他对那些盗贼和杀人犯们说："我是个织工，我编的草席特别值钱。"于是他们给他拿来草叫他编，三天后，他织出了三张草席，他说："把这些草席带到波斯国王的宫殿里，每张草席国王会给你一百枚金币。"就这样，草席被送进了国王的宫殿，国王一眼就认出草席出自儿子之手。他把草席拿给牧羊人的女儿看，说："这些草席是被送进宫里来的，是我失踪了的儿子编的。"牧羊人的女儿拿起草席一张张地仔细审视，从草席的图案里发现了丈夫用波斯文编织的信息，她把这些信息解释给国王听。

祖母说，国王就派许多士兵冲进了盗贼和杀人犯聚集的黑店，杀死了所有的盗贼和杀人犯，把所有的囚犯都解救出来了，国王的儿子也平安地返回了王宫，又可以陪伴他的妻子——牧羊人可爱的小女儿了。他走进王宫与妻子重逢时，降尊纡贵地跪在她面前，抱着她的脚，说："我的爱，因为你的缘故，我才大难不死。"就这样，牧羊人的女儿大大地博得了国王的欢心。

祖母说："现在你明白了人为什么要学一门值得尊敬的手艺了吧？"

我已经心领神会，我说："等我一赚够了钱，就去买把锯子、锤子和一块木板，我要尽心竭力做一把简单的椅子或者一个书架。"

The Shepherd's Daughter

By William Saroyan

It is the opinion of my grandmother, God bless her, that all men should labor. And at the table, a moment ago, she said to me: "You must learn to do some good work, the making of some item useful to man, something out of clay, or out of wood, or metal, or cloth. It is not proper for a young man to be ignorant of an honourable craft. Is there anything you can make? Can you make a simple table, a chair, a plain dish, a rug, a coffee pot? If there anything you can do?"

And my grandmother looked at me with anger. "I know, she said, you are supposed to be a writer, and I suppose you are. You certainly smoke enough cigarettes to be anything, and the whole house is full of the smoke, but you must learn to make solid things, things that can be used, that can be seen and touched."

There was a king of the Persians, said my grandmother, and he had a son, and this son fell in love with a shepherd's daughter. He went to his father and he said, "My Lord, I love a shepherd's daughter, and I would have her for my wife." And the king said, "I am king and you are my son, and when I die you shall be king, how can it be that you would marry the daughter of a shepherd?" And the son said, "My Lord, I do not know but I know that I love this girl and would have her for my queen."

The king saw that his son's love for the girl was from God, and he said, "I will send a message to her." And he called a messenger to him and he said, "Go to the shepherd's daughter and say that my son loves her and would have her for his wife." And the messenger went to the girl and he said, "The king's son loves you and would have you for his wife." And the girl said, "What labor does he do?" And the messenger said, "Why, he is the son of the king; he does no labor." And the girl said, "He must learn to do some labor." And the messenger returned to the king and spoke the words of the shepherd's daughter.

The king said to his son, "the shepherd's daughter wishes you to learn some craft. Would you still have her for your wife?" And the son said, "Yes, I will learn to weave straw rugs." And the boy was taught to weave rugs of straw, in patterns and in colours and with ornamental designs, and at the end of three days he was making very fine straw rugs, and the messenger returned to the shepherd's daughter, and he said, "These rugs of straw are the work of the king's son." And the girl went with the messenger to the king's palace, and she became the wife of the king's son.

One day, said my grandmother, the king's son was walking

through the streets of Baghdad, and he came upon an eating place which was so clean and cool that he entered it and sat at a table.

This place, said my grandmother, was a place of thieves and murderers, and they took the king's son and placed him in a large dungeon where many great men of the city were being held, and the thieves and murderers were killing the fattest of the men and fee ding them to the leanest of them, and making sport of it. The king's son was of the leanest of the men, and it was not known that he was the son of the king of the Persians, so his life was spared, and he said to the thieves and murderers, "I am a weaver of straw rugs and these rugs have great value. " And they brought him straw and asked him to weave and in three days he weaved three rugs, and he said, "Carry these to the palace of the king of the Persians, and for each rug he will give you a hundred gold pieces of money. " And the rugs were carried to the palace of the king, and when the king saw the rugs he saw that they were the work of his son and he took the rugs to the shepherd's daughter and he said, "These rugs were brought to the palace and they are the work of my son who is lost. " And the shepherd's daughter took each rug and looked at it closely and in the design of each rug she saw in the written language of the Persians a message from her husband, and she related this message to the king.

And the king, said my grandmother, sent many soldiers to the place of the thieves and murderers, and the soldiers rescued all the captives and killed all the thieves and murderers, and the king's son was returned safely to the palace of his father, and to the company of his wife, the little shepherd's daughter. And when the boy went into the palace and saw again his wife, he humbled himself before her and he embraced her feet, and he said, "My love, it is because of you that I am alive," and the king was greatly pleased with the shepherd's daughter.

Now, said my grandmother, "do you see why every man should learn an honourable craft?"

I see very clearly, I said, "and as soon as I earn enough money to buy a saw and a hammer and a piece of lumber I shall do my best to make a simple chair or a shelf for books."

动物学校

　　从前，动物们痛下决心一定要采取果断举措来应对"新世界"出现的种种棘手的问题，于是他们开办了一所动物学校，课程内容包括跑步、爬行、游泳和飞行。为了管理简便起见，要求所有动物都要入学，门门功课都要上。

　　鸭子在游泳方面极为出色，事实上比教练还要强。可他的飞行课只得了个及格，跑步课就更差了。正是因为跑得慢，所以放学以后还要留下来继续练习，连游泳课也放弃了。就这样，直到他的蹼状鸭掌被磨得面目全非，游泳课也只得了个及格分数。不过，校方觉得可以接受及格成绩，所以，除了鸭子之外，谁也不为这个问题烦心。

　　兔子在班里是跑得最快的，却因为游泳课要做那么多的化妆工作而神经紧张，精神崩溃。

　　松鼠爬行原本就很出色，却在飞行课上遭到了挫败，因为他的老师要求他从地上而不是从树梢上起飞。由于太投入，他还得了恐高症。最后，他的爬行课得了个及格，跑步课得了个不及格。

　　鹰是一个"问题孩子"，因此受到了严格的管束。在爬行课上，他站在树梢上力挫群雄，一举夺冠，却固执地坚持以自己的方式上树。

　　就这样，一学年学下来，一条变态的鳗鱼不仅游得特别好，还可以跑一段，爬一段，飞一段，所以平均分最高，于是作为学生代表在毕草原狗逃税抗税，声称是因为行政部门没把挖洞和打洞纳入动物学校的课程计划。他们先是把孩子交给獾来教，而后又有土拨鼠和囊地鼠加盟，他们共同创立了一所私立学校，私立学校很成功。

这个寓言有寓意吗？

这个寓言有寓意吗？

业典礼上发言。

　　草原狗逃税抗税，声称是因为行政部门没把挖洞和打洞纳入动物学校的课程计划。他们先是把孩子交给獾来教，而后又有土拨鼠和囊地鼠加盟，他们共同创立了一所私立学校，私立学校很成功。

　　这个寓言有寓意吗？

The Animal School

Once upon a time, the animals decided they must do something heroic to meet the problems of "a new world". So they organized a school. They adopted an activity curriculum consisting of running, climbing, swimming and flying. To make it easier to administer the curriculum, all the animals took all the subjects.

The duck was excellent in swimming, in fact better than his instructor, but he made only passing grades in flying and was very poor in running. Since he was slow in running, he had to stay after school and also drop swimming in order to practice running. This was kept up until his webbed feet were badly worn and he was only average in swimming. But average was acceptable in school, so nobody worried about that except the duke.

The rabbit started at the top of the class in running, but had a nervous breakdown because of so much makeup work in swimming.

The squirrel was excellent in climbing until he developed frustration in the flying class where his teacher made him start from the ground up instead of from the treetop down. He also developed a "charlie horse" from overexertion and then got a C in climbing and a D in running.

The eagle was a problem child and was disciplined severely. In the climbing class he beat all the others to the top of the tree, but insisted on using his own way to get there.

At the end of the year, an abnormal eel that could swim exceedingly well, and also run, climb and fly a little, had the highest average and was valedictorian.

The prairie dogs stayed out of school and fought the tax levy because the administration would not add digging and burrowing to the curriculum. They apprenticed their children to a badger and later joined the groundhogs and gophers to start a successful private school.

Does this fable have a moral?

感情岛

【英】鲍勃·格林汉姆

从前有一个岛，岛上住着所有的感情：欢乐、悲伤、知识，等等，也包括爱。

有一天，所有的感情都得知了一个消息：感情岛即将沉入海底，于是，所有的感情都备船，准备离开。

只有爱留了下来，她要守护天堂岛，直到最后一刻。

岛屿彻底沉入海底的时候，爱知道最后离别的时刻到了。

她开始找人求助。富有恰好在此时乘着一艘大船路过，于是爱问道："富有，我可以搭你的船吗？"

富有回答："对不起，我船上有不少金银财宝，你连立足之地都没有。"

爱决定向坐着一艘华丽的船经过的虚荣求助，爱大声喊道："虚荣，请你帮帮我！""我帮不了你。"虚荣回答，"你浑身上下都湿透了，会把我漂亮的船毁了的。"

接着，爱看到悲伤经过，爱说："悲伤，请你让我跟你一起走。"

悲伤回答："爱，对不起，可我现在只想一个人待着。"

接下来，爱看见了快乐，于是爱大声喊道："快乐，请把我带上。"

可是，快乐太快乐了，甚至都没听见爱的叫声。

爱哭了起来。不一会儿，她听到一个声音说："爱，过来，我会带你。"说话的是一个长者。爱大喜过望，甚至忘了询问长者是谁。他们弃舟登岸以后，长者接着走他的路。爱这才意识到自己亏欠长者太多。

爱接着找到知识问道："帮了我的那位长者是谁呀？"

"是时间。"知识答道。"别人都能帮我却不肯帮，这时为什么时间会出手相助？"爱问道。

知识意味深长地微笑着，异常真挚地回答："因为只有时间才能理解伟大的爱。"

Island of Feelings

By Bob Graham

Once upon a time, there was an island where all the feelings lived: Happiness, Sadness, Knowledge, and all the others, including Love.

One day it was announced to all of the feelings that the island was going to sink to the bottom of the ocean. So all the feelings prepared their boats to leave.

Love was the only one that stayed. She wanted to preserve the island paradise until the last possible moment.

When the island was almost totally under, love decided it was time to leave.

She began looking for someone to ask for help. Just then Richness was passing by in a grand boat. Love asked, "Richness, can I come with you on your boat?"

Richness answered, "I'm sorry, but there is a lot of silver and gold on my boat and there would be no room for you anywhere."

Then Love decided to ask Vanity for help who was passing by in a beautiful vessel. Love cried out, "Vanity, help me please!" "I can't help you," Vanity said, "You are all wet and will damage my beautiful boat."

Next, Love saw Sadness passing by. Love said, "Sadness, please let me go with you."

Sadness answered, "Love, I'm sorry, but, I just need to be alone now."

Then, Love saw Happiness. Love cried out, "Happiness, please take me with you." But Happiness was so overjoyed that he didn't hear Love calling to him.

Love began to cry. Then, she heard a voice say, "Come Love, I will take you with me." It was an elder. Love felt so blessed and overjoyed that she forgot to ask the elder his name. When they arrived on land the elder went on his way. Love realized how much she owed the elder.

Love then found Knowledge and asked, "Who was it that helped me?"

"It was Time," Knowledge answered. "But why did Time help me when no one else would?" Love asked.

Knowledge smiled and with deep wisdom and sincerity, answered, "Because only Time is capable of understanding how great Love is."

七色彩虹的传说

从前，世界上的颜色曾经争吵不休：他们个个都声称自己是最好、最重要、最有用、最受喜爱的颜色。

绿色说："显而易见，我是举足轻重的。我是生命和希望的象征。我被首选成为青草、树叶和树木的颜色——没有了我，所有的动物都会死。到乡村去极目远眺，你就会发现我的颜色是主打色。"

蓝色打断了他的话："你只想到了陆地，却忘记了把天空和海洋都考虑进去。水是生命的根本。天空给予世界空间、和平与宁静。没有我带来的和平，你们都会化作乌有。"

黄色咯咯轻声笑着开了腔："你们都这么一本正经的，是我给世界带来了欢声笑语、快乐和温暖。太阳是黄色的，月亮也是黄色的，连星星都是黄色的。每次你看葵花的时候，会觉得全世界都在向你展开笑颜。没有了我，就没有乐趣。"

橙色成了下一个发泄怒气的："我是健康和力量的颜色。我很稀少，却很珍贵，因为我满足了人类生活的需要。我含有最重要的维生素，想想胡萝卜、南瓜、橘子、芒果和木瓜吧。我并不是总逗留不去，可是每当我在日出和日落时分笼罩天空的时候，相比之下，我惊人的美让全世界都会觉得你们黯然失色。"

红色再也忍无可忍了，他大喊大叫道："我是你们的统治者！我是血液！生命就是血液！我象征着危险和勇敢。我愿意为事业而战。我给火带来血！我是激情、爱情、红玫瑰、罂粟和猩猩木的颜色。没有我，地球会像月亮一样空空如也！"

紫色站直了身子，他身材高大，说起话来口气也很大："我是权贵的颜色。国王、最高领导人、主教总是选择我的颜色，因为我象征着权力和智慧。平民百姓不会质疑我，他们俯首帖耳，洗耳恭听。"

最后，靛青色开了口，比别人都要安静，却跟别人一样斩钉截铁："想想我吧。我是沉默的颜色。你们几乎注意不到我，可是没有我的话，你们都会变得肤浅之极。我象征着思考和反省、黎明和深水。你们需要我来在祈祷和内心的平和中发挥平衡和对比的作用。"

于是，所有的颜色都继续自吹自擂，争吵不休，都想说服别人，证明自己比别人优越。就这样，他们的争吵声越来越大。突然，出现了一道刺眼的闪电，惊天动地！雷声隆隆，震耳欲聋！无情的雨水倾盆而下。所有的颜色都吓得蜷缩下来，相互偎依着寻求安慰。

在一片喧闹声中，雨开口说话了："你们这些愚蠢的颜色，徒自内讧，都想控制别人。难道你们不知道你们各自都是独一无二，与众不同，都有特殊的用途的吗？拉起手，跟我来。"

他们拉起了手，颜色交叠，手儿相牵。雨接着说道："从现在开始，每当雨后，你们每个人都拉出一道大大的弓形的颜色，提醒大家可以和平共处。雨后的彩虹就是希望和未来的象征。"

于是，每当一场好雨清洗世界之后，就会有一道彩虹出现在天空之上，要我们牢记要彼此欣赏。

A Story of the Rainbow

Once upon a time the colors of the world started to quarrel: all claimed that they were the best, the most important, the most useful, the favorite.

GREEN said: "Clearly I am the most important. I am the sign of life and of hope. I was chosen for grass, leaves, trees—without me, all animals would die. Look out over the countryside and you will see that I am in the majority."

BLUE interrupted: "You only think about the Earth, but consider the sky and sea. It is the water that is the basis of life. The sky gives space and peace and serenity. Without my peace, you would all be nothing."

YELLOW chuckled: "You are all so serious. I bring laughter, gaiety, and warmth to the world. The sun is yellow, the moon is yellow, and the stars are yellow. Every time you look at a sunflower, the whole world starts to smile. Without me, there would be no fun."

ORANGE started next to blow her temper: "I am the color of health and strength. I may be scarce but I am precious for I serve the needs of human life. I carry the most important vitamins. Think of carrots, pumpkins, oranges, mangos, and pawpaws. I don't hang around all the time, but when I fill the sky at sunrise or sunset, my beauty is so striking that no one gives another thought to any of you."

RED could stand it no longer. He shouted out: "I am the ruler of all of you! I am blood! Life's blood! I am the color of danger and of bravery. I am willing to fight for a cause. I bring fire to the blood! I am the color of passion and of love, the red rose, the poppy and the poinsettia. Without me, the earth would be as empty as the moon!"

PURPLE rose up to his full height. He was very tall and spoke with great pomp: "I am the color of royalty and power. Kings, chiefs, and bishops have always chosen me for I am a sign of authority and wisdom. People do not question me, they listen and obey."

Finally, INDIGO spoke, much more quietly than all the others, but with just as much determination: "Think of me. I am the color of silence. You hardly notice me, but without me you all become superficial. I represent thought and reflection, twilight and deep water. You need me for balance and contrast, for prayer and inner peace."

And so all the colors went on boasting and quarreling, each convinced of their own superiority. Soon, their quarreling became louder and louder. Suddenly there was a startling flash of bright lightening! Thunder rolled and boomed! Rain started to pour down relentlessly. The colors crouched down in fear drawing close to one another for comfort.

In the midst of the clamor, RAIN began to speak: "You foolish colors, fighting amongst yourselves, each trying to dominate the rest. Don't you know you were each made for a special purpose, unique and different? Join hands with one another and come to me."

Doing as they were told, the colors united and joined hands. The RAIN continued: "From now on, when it rains, each of you will stretch across the sky in a great bow of colors as a reminder that you can all live in peace. The rainbow is a sign of hope for tomorrow."

And so, whenever a good rain washes the world, and a rainbow appears in the sky, let us remember to appreciate one another.

睡丑人

【英】简·约伦

假如你把迈泽蕊拉公主从眼睛、鼻子、嘴一直看到脚，那么，你会承认她是一个美貌动人的公主。然而，在她的内心深处，在你不容易看到的地方，她是周围最卑鄙、最邪恶、最一无是处的公主。她喜欢踩狗，她踢猫，她爱把饼摔在厨师的脸上，她从来没有——就连一次都没有——对厨师说过"谢谢你"和"请"，此外，她还爱说谎。

在这个王国的森林中部，还住着一个可怜的孤儿，名叫其貌不扬简。名副其实，她确实其貌不扬，她的头发短短的，还向下耷拉着，她的鼻子长长的，还向上翻着。就算她的头发不向下耷拉，鼻子不向上翻着，她也不是一个大美人。可是她爱动物，对不认识的老妇人总是很和善。

有一天，迈泽蕊拉公主像平时那样骑着马怒气冲冲地出了宫。她骑啊骑啊骑，虽然头发乱糟糟的，人看上去还是很漂亮。

她一口气骑进了森林中部，不久就迷了路。她跳下马来，狠狠地抽打马，怪马走迷了路。马一声没吭，而是立刻跑回了家。马总是记得回家的路，却不想告诉迈泽蕊拉。就这样，迈泽蕊拉公主在黑暗的森林中迷了路，这使她看起来更漂亮了。

突然，迈泽蕊拉公主被在树下熟睡的一个瘦小的老妇人绊了一下。

当时，在黑暗的树林里的树下睡觉的瘦小的老妇人差不多都是乔装打扮的仙女。迈泽蕊拉也猜出了瘦小的老妇人的身份，可她却满不在乎。她用脚踢着老妇人的屁股，"起来，把我送回家去。"她命令道。

于是，老妇人动作非常迟缓地站了起来——因为屁股此时还疼着呢。她牵着迈泽蕊拉的手。（她只用拇指和中指牵着迈泽蕊拉的手，仙女们对这种公主略知一二。）

她们走啊走，却走进了密林的更深处。在那里，她们发现了一个小小的房子，那就是其貌不扬简的房子，房子不讨人喜欢，地板塌陷，墙壁散发着臭气，阳光灿烂的日子屋顶也漏水。

可是简尽其可能地把房子收拾好。她在门周围种了玫瑰花，小动物们把家跟她安在一起。（可能就是因为这个原因，地板才会塌陷，墙壁才会散发臭气的吧，可是谁也没有怨言。）

"这不是我的家。"迈泽蕊拉用轻蔑的口吻说道。

"也不是我的家。"仙女反唇相讥。

她们没敲门就进了屋，简正好在家，她接口道："这是我的家。"

公主从脚到头，又从头到脚地打量着简。"把我送回家，"迈泽蕊拉说，"作为回报，我会让你当我的仆人。"

其貌不扬简淡淡地微微一笑，这一笑，并没有让她更美丽，也没有让公主的心情更好。"某种回报，"仙女心中暗想，然后说出声来："你若是能把我们两个都送回家，我或许可以挤出一两个愿望来。"

"三个愿望吧，"迈泽蕊拉对仙女说道，"那样的话，我把我们俩送回家。"

其貌不扬简又微笑了，鸟儿们开始歌唱。"我的家就是你们的家。"简说道。

"我喜欢你的风度，"仙女说，"为了这个好的想法，我就给你许三个愿望的机会。"

迈泽蕊拉公主不高兴了，她跺着脚。"再跺，"仙女边说边从口袋里拿出一根松树枝，"我就把你的脚变成石头。"为了使坏，迈泽蕊拉又跺了跺脚，那只脚立刻变成了石头。

其貌不扬简幽幽长叹："我的第一个愿望就是把她的脚变回来。"

仙女做了个鬼脸。"我喜欢你的风度，却不喜欢你的品位，"她对简说道，"不过，愿望就是愿望。"仙女挥动着松树枝。公主抖了抖脚，那只脚不再是石头脚了。

"我想我的脚不过是打了个盹罢了，"迈泽蕊拉说道，她可真是喜欢说谎。"此外，"公主又说，"这么浪费一个愿望是愚蠢的。"

仙女生气了："在还没有人介绍你是何许人也之前，或者在你还不是别人的家庭成员之前，不要骂别人愚蠢。"

"愚蠢，愚蠢，愚蠢！"迈泽蕊拉说道，她不喜欢被人教导怎么做。

"再说一次愚蠢的话，"仙女举起了松树枝，警告道，"我就会让癞蛤蟆从你嘴里跳出来。"

"愚蠢！"迈泽蕊拉大喊大叫，话音未落，一个巨大的癞蛤蟆从她嘴里跳了出来。

"真可爱，"简说着，从地上捡起了癞蛤蟆，"我真的喜欢癞蛤蟆，可是……"

"可是什么？"仙女问道。迈泽蕊拉的嘴没有张开，癞蛤蟆是她最讨厌的动物之一。

"可是，"其貌不扬简说，"我的第二个愿望是让她的嘴里没有癞蛤蟆。"

"她很幸运，嘴里含的不是大象。"仙女咕哝着。她挥了挥松树枝。

迈泽蕊拉慢腾腾地张开了嘴，嘴里除了舌头，没出来其他东西，她用手指着仙女。

迈泽蕊拉看起来很痛苦，这也使得她看上去更美了，"我确实受够啦，"她说，"我想要回家。"她一把抓住了简的胳膊。

"温柔点，温柔点，"老仙女边说边摇着头，"你对魔法不温柔，我们哪里都去不了，谁也不例外。"

"你爱去哪儿就去哪儿，"迈泽蕊拉说，"可是我现在只想回家。"

"睡觉！"仙女喊道，她此时怒发冲冠，已经不记得要温柔了，她使劲地挥舞着松树枝，树枝打到了简家里的墙上。

墙裂了，树枝断了，咒语停止了，还没等简许第三个愿，她们三个都沉沉睡去了。

这就是那种三百年的眠，这就是需要王子的吻才能醒的眠。她们就这样在森林小屋里睡啊睡，在她们熟睡期间，发生了三个半战争，一场瘟疫，更替了六个国王，发明了缝纫机，发现了新大陆，而小屋在密林深处，绝少有王子路过，路过的王子也没有想过去开门。

在一百年快要过去的时候，一个名叫乔乔的王子（是最小的王子的最小的儿子，所以没有什么金银财宝值得一提）进了森林，而天却下起雨来，所以他从小屋墙的豁口走了进去。

他看见了垂到地板上的蜘蛛网里罩着的三个熟睡的女人，其中有一个是美丽的公主。

乔乔是那种爱读神话故事的小伙子，所以知道自己该做什么。可是，因为他是最小的王子的最小的儿子，没有什么值得一提的金银财宝，所以还从来没有吻过任何人。他的母亲除外，也不算；他的父亲还有胡子。

乔乔想，在吻公主之前得练习练习。（此外，他还不知道她愿不愿意嫁给一个没有金银财宝值得一提的王子。乔乔知道公主对这种东西都很在意。）于是，他嘬起嘴唇吻了吻老仙女的鼻子，她闻起来有淡淡的肉桂的味道，他感觉很愉快。

他往简身边挪了挪，嘬起嘴吻了吻她的嘴唇。它闻起来有野花的味道，他大喜过望。他挪到了美丽的公主身边，就在这时，仙女和其貌不扬简醒了过来，乔乔王子的吻已经生效了，仙女拿起了她的松树枝。

简望着王子，忆起了刚才那梦一般的亲吻。"但愿他能爱上我。"她心中轻轻地默念。

"美好的愿望！"仙女自言自语道。她温柔地挥动着两根松树枝。王子看着迈泽蕊拉，迈泽蕊拉正在做一个噩梦，还很享受，虽然在皱眉，却依旧不失美丽。可是乔乔对这种公主太了解了，他有三个外表美丽，内心丑恶的表妹，跟她一模一样。

他想起了野花的味道，于是转过身来对简表白："我爱你，你叫什么名字？"

就这样，他们从此在简的小屋里开始了幸福地生活。王子把屋顶和墙壁修好了，还在隔壁给老仙女盖了幢房子。

朋友们来访的时候，他们把熟睡的公主当作一个话题，有时他们把她立在（她还在熟睡）门廊里，往她的胳膊上搭外套和帽子，可是他们严令禁止任何人把她吻醒，包括他们的三个孩子。

寓意：对付说谎的公主最明智的做法就是让她永远酣睡。

Sleeping Ugly

By Jane Yolen

Princess Miserella was a beautiful princess if you counted her eyes and nose and mouth and all the way down to her toes. But inside, where it was hard to see, she was the meanest, wickedest, and most worthless princess around. She liked stepping on dogs. She kicked kittens. She threw pies in the cook's face. And she never — not even once — said thank you or please. And besides, she told lies.

In that very same kingdom, in the middle of the woods, lived a poor orphan named Plain Jane. She certainly was. Her hair was short and turned down. Her nose was long and tuned up. And even if they had been the other way round, she would not have been a great beauty. But she loved animals, and she was always kind to strange old ladies.

One day Princess Miserella rode out of the palace in a huff. She rode and rode and rode, looking beautiful as always, even with her hair in tangles.

She rode right into the middle of the woods and was soon lost. She got off her horse and slapped it sharply for losing the way. The horse said nothing, but ran right back home. It had known the way back all the time, but it was not about to tell Miserella. So there was the princess, lost in a dark wood. It made her look even prettier.

Suddenly, Princess Miserella tripped over a little old lady asleep under a tree. Now little old ladies who sleep under trees deep in a dark wood are almost always fairies in disguise. Miserella guessed who the little old lady was, but she did not care. She kicked the old lady on the bottoms of her feet. "Get up and take me home," said the princess.

So the old lady got to her feet very slowly — for the bottoms now hurt. She took Miserella by the hand. (She used only her thumb and second finger to hold Miserella's hand. Fairies knew quite a bit about that kind of princess.)

They walked and walked even deeper into the wood. There they found a little house. It was Plain Jane's house. It was dreary. The floors sank. The walk stank. The roof leaked even on sunny days.

But Jane made the best of it. She planted roses around the door. And little animals and birds made their home with her. (That may be why the floors sank and the walls stank, but no one explained.)

"This is not my home," said Miserella with a sniff.

"Nor mine," said the fairy.

They walked in without knocking, and there was Jane. "It is mine," she said.

The princess looked at Jane, down and up, up and down. "Take me home, " said Miserella, "and as a reward I will make you my maid."

Plain Jane smiled a thin little smile. It did not improve her looks or the princess's mood. "Some reward, " said the fairy to herself. Out loud she said, "If you could take both of us home, I could probably squeeze out a wish or two."

"Make it three, " said Miserella to the fairy, "and I'll get us home."

Plain Jane smiled again. The birds began to sing. "My home is your home, " said Jane.

"I like your manners," said the fairy. "And for that good thought, I'll give three wishes to you."

Princess Miserella was not pleased. She stamped her foot. "Do that again," said the fairy, taking a pine wand from her pocket, "and I'll turn your foot to stone." Just to be mean, Miserella stamped her foot again. It turned to stone.

Plain Jane sighed. "My first wish is that you change her foot back."

The fairy made a face. "I like your manners, but not your taste, " she said to Jane. "Still, a wish is a wish." The fairy moved the wand. The princess shook her foot. It was no longer made of stone.

"Guess my foot fell asleep for a moment, " said Miserella. She really liked to lie. "Besides, " the princess said, "that was a stupid way to waste a wish."

The fairy was angry. "Do not call someone stupid unless you have been properly introduced, " she said, "or are a member of the family."

"Stupid, stupid, stupid！" said Miserella. She hated to be told what to do.

"Say stupid again," warned the fairy, holding up her wand, "and I will make toads come out of your mouth."

"Stupid！" shouted Miserella. As she said it, a great big toad dropped out of her mouth.

"Cute, " said Jane, picking up the toad, "and I do like toads, but..."

"But？" asked the fairy. Miserella did not open her mouth. Toads were among her least favorite animals.

"But, " said Plain Jane, "my second wish is that you get rid of the mouth toads."

"She's lucky it wasn't mouth elephants, " mumbled the fairy. She waved the pine wand. Miserella opened her mouth slowly. Nothing came out but her tongue. She pointed it at the fairy.

Princess Miserella looked miserable. That made her look beautiful, too. "I definitely have had enough, " she said. "I want to go home." She grabbed Plain Jane's arm.

"Gently, gently, " said the old fairy, shaking her head. "If you are not gentle with magic, none of us will go anywhere."

"You can go where you want, " said Miserella, "but here is

only one place I want to go."

"To sleep！" said the fairy，who was now much too mad to remember to be gentle. She waved her wand so hard she hit the wall of Jane's house.

The wall broke. The wand broke. The spell broke. And before Jane could make her third wish，all three of them were asleep.

It was one of those famous hundred-year-naps that need a prince and a kiss to end them. So they slept and slept in the cottage in the wood. They slept through three and a half wars，one plague，six new kings，the invention of the sewing machine，and the discovery of a new continent. The cottage was deep in the woods so very few princes passed by. And none of the ones who did even tried the door.

At the end of one hundred years a prince named Jojo（who was the youngest son of a youngest son and so had no gold or jewels or property to speak of）came into the woods. It began to rain，so he stepped into the cottage over the broken wall.

He saw three women asleep with spider webs holding them to the floor. One of them was a beautiful princess.

Being the kind of young man who read fairy tales，Jojo knew just what to do. But because he was the youngest son of a youngest son，with no gold or jewels or property to speak of，he had never kissed anyone before，except his mother，which didn't count，and his father，who had a beard.

Jojo thought he should practice before he tried kissing the princess.

（He also wondered if she would like marrying a prince with no property or gold or jewels to speak of. Jojo knew with princesses that sort of thing really matters.） So he puckered up his lips and kissed the old fairy on the nose. It was quite pleasant. She smelled slightly of cinnamon.

He moved on to Jane. He puckered up his lips and kissed her on the mouth. It was delightful. She smelled of wild flowers. He moved on to the beautiful princess. Just then the fairy and Plain Jane woke up. Prince Jojo's kisses had worked. The fairy picked up the pieces of her wand.

Jane looked at the prince and remembered the kiss as if it were a dream. "I wish he loved me，" she said softly to herself.

"Good wish！" said the fairy to herself. She waved the two pieces of wand gently. The prince looked at Miserella，who was having a bad dream and enjoying it. Even frowning she was beautiful. But Jojo knew that kind of princess. He had three cousins just like her. Pretty on the outside. Ugly within.

He remembered the smell of wild flowers and turned back to Jane. "I love you，" he said. "What's your name？"

So they lived happily ever after in Jane's cottage. The prince fixed the roof and the wall and built a house next door for the old fairy.

They used the sleeping princess as a conversation piece when friends came to visit. Or sometimes they stood her up （still fast asleep） in the hallway and let her hold coats and hats. But they never let anyone kiss her awake, not even their children, who numbered three.

Moral: Let sleeping princesses lie or lying princesses sleep, whichever seems wisest.

小青蛙

　　从前，有一群小青蛙计划搞一次赛跑，赛跑的终点是一座特别高的高塔塔尖。塔底下已经聚集了一大群人，都是来观看比赛，给参赛者助威的。

　　比赛开始了……

　　实话实说，这么一大群人里，没有一个人相信小小的青蛙能爬到塔顶的。你能听到这样那样的说法，譬如"哦，路太难走啦！""它们绝对爬不上去。""它们要想爬上去，门儿都没有，塔太高了嘛！"小青蛙们开始一个接一个地溃退，只剩那些新鲜劲儿还没过的小青蛙，还在全速前进，越爬越高。

　　人们还在大喊大叫："太难啦！谁都爬不上去！"又有一些小青蛙疲惫不堪地放弃了，但是，有一个小青蛙越爬越高，越爬越高。这个小青蛙不肯放弃。最后，所有的小青蛙都放弃了登塔比赛，只有这个小青蛙，在历尽千辛万苦之后，成为唯一登上塔顶的小青蛙。

　　比赛结束以后，其余的小青蛙自然都想知道这只小青蛙是怎么排除万难做到的，一个赛手问这个小青蛙它不达目的，决不罢休的必胜的力量从何而来。你猜怎么着？他发现这个获胜的小青蛙原来是个聋子。

　　这个故事的寓意是：千万不要听从别人的负面意见、悲观意见，因为这样会把你内心深处最美好的美梦和愿景夺走。

永远不要忘了：话语是有力量的，因为你听什么话，看什么书，都会影响到你的行为。所以，态度永远要积极。而最要紧的是，当人们告诫说你无法实现你的梦想的时候，要装聋作哑，充耳不闻。要永远坚信：我能行！

The Tiny Frog

Once upon a time there was a bunch of tiny frogs who arranged a running competition. The goal was to reach the top of a very high tower. A big crowd had gathered around the tower to see the race and cheer on the contestants.

The race began...

Honestly, no one in the crowd really believed that the tiny frogs would reach the top of the tower. You heard statements such as "Oh, WAY too difficult!" "They will NEVER make it to the top." "Not a chance that they will succeed. The tower is too high!" The tiny frogs began collapsing, one by one. Except for those, who in a fresh tempo, were climbing higher and higher.

The crowd continued to yell, "It is too difficult! No one will make it!" More tiny frogs got tired and gave up. But ONE continued higher and higher and higher. This one wouldn't give up! At the end, everyone else had given up climbing the tower. Except for the one tiny frog that, after a big effort, was the only one who reached the top.

Then all of the other tiny frogs naturally wanted to know how this one frog managed to do it. A contestant asked the tiny frog how he had found the strength to succeed and reach the goal. Guess what？ It turned out that the winner was DEAF.

Moral of this story：Never listen to other people's tendencies to be negative or pessimistic，because they take your most wonderful dreams and wishes away from you — the ones you have in your heart.

Always think of the power that words have，because everything you hear and read will affect your actions. Therefore，ALWAYS BE POSITIVE. And above all，be DEAF when people tell you that you cannot fulfill your dreams. Always believe：I can do this！

唯我论者

　　沃尔特·B. 耶和华，我无须向主谢罪，因为耶和华确实是主人公的姓。他的一生都是个唯我论者。也许您恰好不知道这个词，那么，就让找来解释一下，唯我论者就是这样的一种人：他认为除了他本人之外，万事万物其实并不存在，别人以及整个宇宙只存在于他的想象之中，一旦他停止了想象，一切就都不复存在了。

　　有一天，沃尔特·B. 耶和华开始实践他的唯我论。在短短的一周时间里，他的太太与人私奔，他丢了运务员的饭碗，为了阻止一只企图横穿他家门前小路的黑猫，他追赶时还摔断了腿。

　　他躺在医院的病床上，心中暗下决心，要结束这一切。

　　他向窗外望去，凝视着繁星点点，他希望繁星不复存在，天空上繁星就当真消失了。然后，他希望其他人也不复存在，于是，这家医院霎时间变得寂静异常。接着，整个世界也不复存在了，他发觉自己悬浮在虚空里。他轻而易举地去除了自己的身体，现在只剩下最后一步了，那就是让自己不复存在。

　　他这样做了，却没有做到。

　　他想，奇怪，莫非唯我论者也有局限？

　　"有。"一个声音回答道。

　　"你是谁？"沃尔特·B. 耶和华问。

"我就是创造出你想脱离的宇宙的那个人，而现在，你已经取我而代之了……"一声幽幽长叹。"……我终于可以不复存在，寻找我的湮没，由你来接替我的位置啦。"

"可是……我怎么才能不复存在呢？你知道，这正是我想要做的。"

"知道，我知道。"那个声音说道。"你必须像我做过的那样，去创造一个宇宙，然后等待，直到那个世界里某个人信奉了你所信奉的，并且也愿意进入虚无。这样，你才可以退位，由那个人接替你。那么，再见吧。"

就这样，那个声音销声匿迹了。

沃尔特·B. 耶和华孤零零地一个人留在虚无之中，他只有一件事可做：创造天和地。

此举耗时七天。

Solipsist

Walter B. Jehovah, for whose name I make no apology since it really was his name, had been a solipsist all his life. A solipsist, in case you don't happen to know the word, is one who believes that he himself is the only thing that really exists, that other people and the universe in general exist only in his imagination, and that if he quits imagining them they would cease to exist.

One day Walter B. Jehovah became a practicing solipsist. Within a week his wife had run away with another man; he'd lost his job as a shipping clerk and he had broken his leg chasing a black cat to keep it from crossing his path.

He decided, in his bed at the hospital, to end it all.

Looking out the window, staring up at the stars, he wished them out of existence, and they weren't there anymore. Then he wished all other people out of existence and the hospital became strangely quiet even for a hospital. Next, the world, and he found himself suspended in void. He got rid of his body quite as easily and then took the final step of willing himself out of existence.

Nothing happened.

Strange, he thought, can there be a limit to solipsism?

"Yes," a voice said.

"Who are you?" Walter B. Jehovah asked.

"I am the one who created the universe which you had just willed out of existence. And now that you have taken my place" — There was a deep sigh, "—I can finally cease my own existence, find oblivion, and let you take over."

"But—how can I cease to exist? That's what I'm trying to do, you know."

"Yes, I know," said the voice. "You must do it the same way I did. Create a universe. Wait until somebody in it really believes what you believed and wills it out of existence. Then you can retire and let him take over. Good-bye now."

And the voice was gone.

Walter B. Jehovah was alone in the void and there was only one thing he could do. He created the heaven and the earth.

It took him seven days.

死神教父

【德】雅各布·格林　威廉·格林

　　从前有个穷人，他有十二个孩子，为了填饱这十二张嘴，穷人没日没夜地干活。适逢第十三个孩子出生，穷人痛苦难当，一筹莫展，情急之下跑到大路上求遇到的第一个人做这个孩子的教父。走过来的第一个人是上帝，他对穷人心头的重负洞若观火，所以对他说道："可怜的人，我怜悯你，我要把令郎放到洗礼盆里抱着，我会照顾他，让他在人世间快乐地生活。""你是谁？""我是上帝。""那我可不愿意让你做孩子的教父，你让富人应有尽有，却让穷人饥肠辘辘。"穷人就是这么说的，因为他不理解上帝区分贫富的高明之处。他背弃了上帝，转过身来继续往前走。第二个走过来的人是魔鬼。魔鬼问道："你想要什么？如果让我做令郎的教父的话，我会给他金子，他想要多少，我就给他多少。此外，还要给他人世间的一切欢乐。""你是谁？""我是魔鬼。""那我可不想让你做孩子的教父，你总是欺骗误导人类。"穷人又接着往前走，这时，一个腿又细又长的人大踏步地迎了上来，"让我做孩子的教父吧。"那个人说道。"你是谁？""我是死神，众生在我面前一律平等。"那个人回答。"你正是我要找的人，你对穷人和富人一视同仁，你就是犬子的教父了。""我会使令郎名利双收，因为有我这样的朋友的人什么都不缺。"那个人说道。"下星期日举行洗礼，请准时光临。"穷人邀请道。死神果然依约而来，事实证明，他是个完美的理想教父。

孩子长到了成人的年龄，死神教父有一天把他从家里领出来，带进了森林。死神指着林中的一株药草说道："这就是你的洗礼礼物，我要把你变成一个名医。每当你出诊的时候，我就会出现在你身旁，倘若我站在病人的头上，你就可以放心大胆地说能医好他，然后再给他一点这种药草，他就能康复；可是，倘若我站在病人脚上的话，你就一定要说他没希望了，世上的医生都医不好他。注意，不要违背我的意志，否则你会倒霉的。"

不久，这个年轻人就成了声震寰宇的第一大名医，人们这样传颂着他的美名："他医术高明，对病情一望便知，对病人一治即愈。"人们从四面八方赶来请他出诊，给了他那么多的钱，于是他很快就成了阔佬。说来也巧，国王也病了，于是传他进宫，看国王会不会康复。他来到国王的床前，看到死神站在患病的国王的脚下，说明世上的药草都无济于事。医生想：如果这次，就这一次，我能骗过死神，该有多好！我知道他会生气的，可我是他的教子呀，他一定会睁一只眼闭一只眼的，我要冒一次险，碰碰运气。于是他抬起国王，把他的头和脚倒换了方向，这样一来，死神就站在他的头上了。然后，医生给国王服了些药草，国王感觉好起来，很快就安然无恙了。可是，死神来到医生面前，他面色阴沉，满脸怒容，竖起食指威胁道："你骗了我。因为你是我的教子，我这次且放过你，不过，如果你敢故技重施的话，那就是自己把头往绞索里面伸，到了那个时候，我要带走的就是你啦。"

此后不久，国王的独生女儿患了重病，国王日夜哭泣，哭瞎了眼睛，他昭告天下：谁能把公主从死神手里夺回来，谁就可以迎娶公主，继承王位。医生来到公主的床前，看到死神站在她的脚上。他此时本应该想起教父的警告，可一看到公主的绝世美貌，一想到成为她丈夫的幸福，他就昏了头，把教父的警告丢进了风里。死神怒气冲冲地看着他，举起一只手来，用瘦骨嶙峋的拳头威胁着，医生全都没看见。他抬起患病的公主，把她的头放在原来脚所在的位置，又给她服用了一些药草，她的脸上立刻现出了红晕，获得了新生。

　　看到自己再次受骗，失去了财产，死神迈着两条长腿，大踏步地走到医生面前，说道："都是你干的好事，现在该轮到你了。"随即用冰凉的手指狠狠地抓住医生，医生根本没有招架的能力，被带到了一个地下洞穴里。医生看到地下洞穴里有成千上万根蜡烛，一排又一排，无边无际，有些蜡烛很大，有些蜡烛中等，其余的蜡烛很小，每隔一会儿，就会有一些蜡烛燃尽，还会有一些蜡烛亮起来，看起来小火苗好像在蹦来蹦去，变换不停。死神解释道："看吧，这些就是人类的生命之烛，大烛是孩子们的，中烛是正当盛年的已婚夫妇的，小烛是特别老的老人的。然而有时孩子和年轻人也只有小烛。""让我看看我的生命之烛吧。"医生说道，想象那一定是大烛中的一个，不料死神却指着一根即将燃尽小小的残烛说："在这里。"医生惊恐地哀求道："啊，亲爱的教父，给我点根新的吧，看在我的面子上，点吧，这样，我就可以享受生活，君临天下，迎娶美丽的公主了。""我做不到，旧烛燃尽才能点燃新烛。""那就把旧烛放在一根新烛上，这样，旧烛燃尽以后新烛还会继续燃下去。"医生哀哀求告，死神装作答应了似的伸出手去够一根高高的新烛，不过，因为他蓄意报复，所以做得笨手笨脚，结果撞翻了那根残烛。火苗熄灭了，医生扑倒在地，落到了死神手中。

Godfather Death

By Jakob Grimm and Wilhelm Grimm

A poor man had twelve children and worked night and day just to get enough bread for them to eat. Now when the thirteenth came into the world, he did not know what to do and in his misery ran out onto the great highway to ask the first person, he met to be godfather. The first to come along was God, and he already knew what it was that weighed on the man's mind and said, "Poor man, I pity you. I will hold your child at the font and I will look after it and make it happy upon earth." "Who are you?" asked the man. "I am God."

"Then I don't want you for a godfather," the man said. "You give to the rich and let the poor go hungry." That was how the man talked because he did not understand how wisely God shares out wealth and poverty, and thus he turned from the Lord and walked on. Next came. The Devil and said, "What is it you want? If you let me be godfather to your child, I will give him gold as much as he can use, and all the pleasures of the world besides." "Who are you?" asked the man. "I am the Devil." "Then I don't want you for a godfather, " said the man. "You deceive and mislead mankind." He walked on and along came spindle-legged Death striding toward him and said, "Take me as godfather." The man asked, "Who are you? " "I am Death who makes all men equal." Said the man, "Then you're the one for me; you take rich and poor without distinction. You shall be godfather." Answered Death, "I will make your child rich and famous, because the one who has me for a friend shall want for nothing." The man said, "Next Sunday is the baptism. Be there in good time." Death appeared as he had promised and made a perfectly fine godfather.

When the boy was of age, the godfather walked in one day, told him to come along, and led him out into the woods. He showed him an herb which grew there and said, "This is your christening gift. I shall make you into a famous doctor. When you are called to a patient's bedside I will appear and if I stand at the sick man's head you can boldly say that you will cure him and if you give him some of this herb he will recover. But if I stand at the sick man's feet, then he is mine, and you must say there is no help for him and no doctor on this earth could save him. But take care not to use the herb against my will or it could be the worse for you."

It wasn't long before the young man had become the most famous doctor in the whole world. "He looks at a patient and right away he knows how things stand, whether he will get better or if he's going to die." That is what they said about him, and from near and far the people came, took him to see the sick, and gave him so much money he became a rich man. Now it happened! that the king fell ill. The doctor was summoned to say if he was going to get well. When he came to the bed, there stood Death at the feet of the sick man, so that no herb on earth could have done him airy good. If I could only just this once outwit, Death! thought the doctor. He'll be annoyed, I know, but I am his godchild and he's sure to turn a blind eye. I'll take my chance. And so he lifted the sick man and laid him the other way around so that Death was standing at his head. Then he gave him some of the herb and the king began to feel better and was soon in perfect health. But Death came toward the doctor, his face dark and angry, threatened him with raised forefinger, and said "You have tricked me. This time I will let it pass because you are my godchild, but if you ever dare do such a thing again, you put your own head in the noose and it is you I shall carry away with me."

Soon after that, the king's daughter lapsed into a deep illness. She was his only child, he wept day and night until his eyes failed him and he let it be known that whoever saved the princess from death should become her husband and inherit the crown. When the doctor came to the sick girl's bed, he saw Death at her feet. He ought to have remembered his godfather's warning, but the great beauty of the princess and the happiness of becoming her husband so bedazzled him that he threw caution to the winds, nor did he see Death's angry glances and how he lifted his hand in the air and threatened him with his bony fist. He picked the sick girl up and laid her head where her feet had lain, then he gave her some of the herb and at once her cheeks reddened and life stirred anew.

When Death saw himself cheated of his property the second time, he strode toward the doctor on his long legs and said, "It is all up with you, and now it is your turn," grasped him harshly with his ice-cold hand so that the doctor could not resist, and led him to an underground cave, and here he saw thousands upon thousands of lights burning. in rows without end, some big, some middle-sized, others small. Every moment some went out and others lit up so that the little flames seemed to be jumping here and there in perpetual exchange. "Look," said Death, "these are the life lights of mankind. The big ones belong to children, the middle-sized ones to married couples in their best years, the little ones belong to very old people. Yet children and the young often have only little lights." "Show me my life light," said the doctor, imagining that it must be one of the big ones. Death pointed to a little stub threatening to go out and said, "Here it is." "Ah, dear godfather," said the terrified doctor, "light me a new one, do it, for my sake, so that I may enjoy my life and become king and marry the beautiful princess." "I cannot," answered Death. "A light must go out before a new one lights up."

"Then set the old on top of a new one so it can go on burning when the first is finished," begged the doctor. Death made as if to grant his wish, reached for a tall new taper, but because he wanted revenge he purposely fumbled and the little stub fell over and went out. Thereupon the doctor sank to the ground and had himself fallen into the hands of death.

末日审判

【捷克】卡雷尔·卡佩克

　　库格勒的灵魂离开身体以后来到了宇宙以外的另一个世界，那里灰蒙蒙的，无边无际，一片荒芜，无法回避的末日审判终于开始了。库格勒被带上了天堂的法庭，法庭内的设施非常简单，与人世间如出一辙，只有一个例外，那就是没有证人席，其中的缘由到时候就会一目了然了。三个法官年事已高，清一色道貌岸然、令人生厌的嘴脸。库格勒按照千篇一律的常规回答："费迪南德·库格勒，无业，生于某年某月某日，死于……"说到这里，看得出库格勒记不起死的日子了。

　　"申明有罪还是无罪？"庭长问道。

　　"无罪。"库格勒执拗地回答。

　　"带第一个证人。"法官叹了口气。

　　库格勒的对面出现了一个气宇非凡的老先生，他脸上长着络腮胡子，身穿缀有金色星星的蓝色长袍，神态庄严肃穆。

　　他一进来，法官们就全体起立，库格勒虽然不情愿，却也鬼使神差地跟着站了起来，老先生坐下以后，法官们方才落座。

　　"证人，"法官开始讲话，"无所不知的上帝，本庭请您来为费迪南德·库格勒一案作证，因为您是最高真理的化身，因此无须起誓。

为了保证以下程序得以顺利进行，我们谨请您针对本案而谈——除非与本案有关，不涉及具体细节。你，库格勒，不要打断证人的话，他无所不知，抵赖没有用。现在，证人，请吧。"说完，主持法官摘下眼镜，舒舒服服地趴在桌子上，最老的那个法官蜷缩起身体也准备睡一觉，负责记录的天使打开了花名册。

上帝轻轻地咳嗽了一声开了腔："好的。费迪南德·库格勒是工人子弟，从小就是一个桀骜不驯的坏小孩，他非常爱母亲，却不会表达，这也是他叛逆难驯性格形成的原因。年轻人，谁见了你都烦！还记得吗？你偷了公证人花园里的玫瑰，你爸爸要打你的屁股，你却把他的大拇指给咬了。"

"玫瑰是为了收税人的女儿伊玛采的。"库格勒辩解道。

"我知道，"上帝说，"伊玛当时才七岁，你知道她后来怎么样了吗？"

"不知道。"

"她嫁给了奥斯卡，就是那个厂主的儿子，她后来却死于难产。你记得鲁迪·扎鲁巴吗？"

"他怎么样了？"

"哟！他参加了海军，后来在庞贝的一场事故中丧生。你们俩当时是全城最坏的孩子，你，费迪南德·库格勒，在十岁以前还偷盗，说谎成性，还跟老格里布这样游手好闲、靠施舍活命的酒鬼混在一起，当然，你也常常把自己的饭拿去与他分享。"

庭长以手示意这些是题外话，可库格勒却迟迟疑疑地问道："那……他的女儿怎么样了？"

"你是说玛丽吗？"上帝反问道，"她十四岁就嫁了人，二十岁就去世了，在临终前的那段痛苦的日子里，她一直在思念你。你十四岁的时候，也差不多成了酒鬼，经常离家出走，你父亲因此心力交瘁，郁郁而终，你母亲也几乎哭瞎了眼。你给家里带来了不好的名誉，你漂亮的妹妹玛莎一直没能嫁出去，哪个小伙子也不愿意登小偷家的门。她现在依然是孤身一人，因为生活所迫，每天缝衣到深夜，她节衣缩食，身心憔悴，那些以恩人自居的顾客还伤害她的自尊心。"

库格勒羞愧难当，低下了头。

庭长把滑到鼻子上的眼镜扶上去，态度温和地说："证人，咱们应该涉及本案了，被告承认犯有杀人罪了吗？"

听了这话，证人点了点头："他杀了九个人。第一次是在一次口角中发生的，他因此而被捕入狱，在服刑期间彻底变坏了；第二个受害者是他不忠的情人，他因此被判死刑，他却越狱逃跑了；第三个是他抢劫的一个老头；第四个是一个守夜人；第五个和第六个是一对吝啬的老夫妇；第七个是一个美国人，他的同胞；第八个是个路人，碰巧遇上库格勒在逃避警察的追捕，还因为患骨膜炎而痛苦不堪，神志不清。第九个是个警察，他和库格勒同时开枪打死了对方。"

"被告的杀人动机是什么？"庭长问道。

"跟其他杀人犯一样，"上帝答道，"都是出于愤怒和对金钱的贪欲，既有故意杀人，也有过失杀人，有时候就是图一时之快，逞一时之能，有的时候是迫不得已，出于需要。不管怎样，他还是一个慷慨大方的人，常常帮助别人，对女人很和善，对动物很温柔，还很重诺守信。我是不是把他做的好事也说一说呢？"

"谢谢，不必了。"庭长说道，"被告还有什么为自己辩护的吗？"

"没有。"库格勒诚心诚意、漫不经心地回答。

"本庭将认真审理此案。"庭长宣布道，然后，三个法官退了庭。法庭上只剩下上帝和库格勒。

"他们是谁？"库格勒指着刚刚离开的人发问道。

"和你一样，也是人，"上帝答道，"是人间的法官，也是天堂的法官。"

库格勒咬着指甲，"我还以为……我的意思是，虽然我从来没有认真想过，可我猜法官是您，因为……"

"因为我是上帝，"那位高贵的绅士总结道，"但你不明白吗？就是因为我无所不知，所以不可能是法官。"

"不好意思，"库格勒壮着胆子说，"您忘了我在芝加哥杀的那个废物特迪了。"

"怎么会忘？"上帝回答道，"他缓了过来，现在还健在。我知道他告过密，不过，他在其他方面却是非常好的人，特别爱孩子，你不应该把任何人视为彻底的一文不值。"

"可我还是不明白，您为什么不是法官呢？"库格勒若有所思地问道。

"因为假如一个法官对一切都了然于胸，绝对清楚，那他就会理解一切，他的心就会痛苦，他就无法坐在审判席上，我也不例外。正如你所看到的那样，这些法官只知道你犯下的罪行，我却知道你的一切，一个完整的库格勒，所以我当不了法官。"

"可是，为什么他们……要用这些人间的法官当天堂的法官呢？"

"因为人类属于人类，我只是证人。人类不配由神来审判，只能由同类来审判，而我不过是个证人而已，相信我，库格勒，理应如此。"

就在这时，三个法官返回法庭，庭长语气沉重地宣布："本庭宣布，费迪南德·库格勒因多次一级谋杀、误杀、抢劫和蔑视法律、非法携带武器、盗窃玫瑰花行为，被判处终身地狱监禁，立即执行。"

"下一个案子：弗兰克·托兰斯。"

"被告到庭了吗？"

The Last Judgment

By Karel Capek

When Kugler's soul left his body, the next world—a world beyond space, grey, and infinitely desolate. At length the inevitable Last Judgment got around to Kugler. Kugler was brought before a special court of three judges before a jury. The courtroom was furnished simply, almost like courtrooms on earth, with this one exception: there was no provision for swearing in witness. In time, however, the reason for this will become apparent. The judges were old and worthy councilors with austere, bored faces. Kugler complied with the usual tedious formalities: "Kugler Ferdinand, unemployed, born on such and such a date, died..." at this point it was shown Kugler didn't know the date of his own death.

"Do you plead guilty or not guilty?" asked the presiding judge.

"Not guilty," said Kugler obdurately.

"Bring in the first witness," the judge sighed.

Opposite Kugler appeared an extraordinary gentleman, stately, bearded, and clothed in a blue robe strewn with golden stars.

At his entrance, the judges arose. Even Kugler stood up, reluctant but fascinated. Only when the old gentleman took a seat did the judges again sit down.

"Witness," began the presiding judge, "omniscient God, this court has summoned you in order to hear your testimony in the case against Kugler Ferdinand. As you are the supreme truth, you need not take the oath. In the interest of the proceedings, however, we ask you to keep to the subject at hand rather than branch out into particulars— unless they have a bearing on this case. And you, Kugler, don't interrupt the witness. He knows everything, so there's no use denying anything. And now. Witness, if you would please begin." That said, the presiding judge took off his spectacles and leaned comfortably on the bench before him, evidently in preparation for a long speech by the Witness. The oldest of the three judges nestled down in sleep. The recording angel opened the Book of Life.

God, the Witness, coughed lightly and began: "Yes. Kugler Ferdinand, son of a factory worker, was a bad, unmanageable child from his earliest days. He loved his mother dearly, but was unable to show it, this made him unruly and defiant. Young man, you irked everyone! Do you remember how you bit your father on the thumb when he tried to spank you? You had stolen a rose from the notary's garden."

"The rose was for Irma, the tax collector's daughter," Kugler said.

"I know, " said God. "Irma was seven years old at that time. Did you ever hear what happened to her? "

"No, I didn't."

"She married Oscar, the son of the factory owner. But she died of a miscarriage. You remember Rudy Zaruba? "

"What happened to him? "

"Why, he joined the navy and died accidentally in Bombay. You two were the worst boys in the whole town. Kugler Ferdinand, was a thief before his tenth year and an inveterate liar. He kept bad company, too: old Gribble, for instance, a drunkard and an idler, living on handouts. Nevertheless, Kugler shared many of his own meals with Gribble."

The presiding judge motioned with his hand, as if much of this was perhaps unnecessary, but Kugler himself asked hesitantly, "And... what happened to his daughter? "

"Mary? " asked God. "She lowered herself considerably. In her fourteenth year she married. In her twentieth year she died, remembering you in the agony of her death. By your fourteenth year you were nearly a drunkard yourself, and you often ran away from home. Your father's death came about from grief and worry; your mother's eyes faded from crying. You bought dishonor to your home, and your sister, your pretty sister Martha, never married. No young man would come calling at the home of a thief. She's still living alone and in poverty, sewing until late each night. Scrimping has exhausted her, and patronizing customers hurt her pride."

Kugler bent his head, overcome by this revelation.

But the presiding judge fitted his spectacles back on his nose, and said mildly, "Witness, we are obliged to get on with the case. Has the accused committed murder?"

Here the Witness nodded his head. "He murdered nine people. The first one he killed in a brawl, and it was during his prison term for his crime that he became completely corrupted. The second victim was his unfaithful sweetheart. For that he was sentenced to death, but he escaped. The third was an old man whom he robbed. The fourth was a night watchman. The fifth and sixth victims were an old married couple. The seventh man he killed in America, a countryman of his. The eighth man was merely a passerby who happened to be in Kugler's way when Kugler was trying to outrun the police. At that time Kugler had periostitis and was delirious from the pain. The ninth and last was the policeman who killed Kugler exactly when Kugler shot him."

"And why did the accused commit murder?" asked the presiding judge.

"For the same reasons others have," answered God. "Out of anger or desire for money, both deliberately and accidentally—some with pleasure, others from necessity. However, he was generous and often helpful. He was kind to women, gentle with animals, and kept his word. Am I to mention his good deeds?"

"Thank you," said the presiding judge, "but it isn't necessary. Does the accused have anything to say in his own defense?"

"No," Kugler replied with honest indifference.

"The judges of this court will now take this matter under advisement," declared the presiding judge, and the three of them withdrew. Only God and Kugler remained in the courtroom.

"Who are they?" asked Kugler, indicating with his head the men who just left.

"People like you," answered God. "They were judges on earth, so they're judges here as well."

Kugler nibbled his fingertips. "I expected...I mean, I never really thought about it. But I figured you would judge since..."

"Since I'm God," finished the stately gentleman. "But that's just it, don't you see? Because I know everything, I can't possibly judge."

"Excuse me," Kugler ventured, "but you forgot about that good-for-nothing Teddy I shot in Chicago."

"Not at all," God said. "He recovered and is alive this very minute. I know he's an informer, but otherwise he's a very good man and terribly fond of children. You shouldn't think of any person as being completely worthless."

"But I still don't understand why you aren't the judge," Kugler said thoughtfully.

"Because my knowledge is infinite. If judges knew everything, absolutely everything, then they would also understand everything. Their hearts would ache. They couldn't sit in judgment — and neither can I. As it is, they know only about your crimes. I know all about you. The entire Kugler. And that's why I cannot judge."

"But why are they judging... the same people who were judges on earth?"

"Because man belongs to man. As you see, I'm only the witness. Believe me, Kugler, this is the way it should be. Man isn't worthy of divine judgment. He deserves to be judged only by other men."

At that moment, the three returned from their deliberation. In heavy tones the presiding judge announced, "For repeated crimes of first-degree murder, manslaughter, robbery, disrespect for the law, illegally carrying weapons, and for the theft of a rose; Kugler Ferdinand, is sentenced to lifelong punishment in hell. The sentence is to begin immediately."

"Next case please: Torrance Frank."

"Is the accused present in court?"

两个狙击手

【爱尔兰】利亚姆·欧弗拉瑟蒂

　　漫长的六月微光渐渐在夜幕中消退，都柏林笼罩在黑暗中，从朵朵轻云中透出的微光笼罩着一排排街道和利弗河黑黝黝的河面，这是即将到来的黎明之光。重型大炮在四法院周围轰鸣，机关枪声和步枪声像空寂农场里的狗吠声似的一阵接一阵地响起，划破了城市的夜空。共和党人和自由党人正在打内战。

　　个共和党人的狙击手趴在奥康奈尔桥附近的一个屋顶上观察着，他的身旁放了一支步枪，肩上挎了一副战地望远镜，他非常年轻的面庞还是学生模样，身体瘦削得像一个苦行僧，可是他的眼睛却闪着狂热的寒光，这是一对深沉的、若有所思的双眼，对死亡已经司空见惯。

　　他在狼吞虎咽地吃三明治，从早晨到现在他还没吃过东西，他太兴奋了。吃完三明治，他从口袋里掏出威士忌酒瓶喝了一小口，又把酒瓶放回口袋。他顿了顿，考虑着是否应该冒险抽口烟。会很危险，黑灯瞎火的，敌人会发现火光，敌人也在观察哩。最后，他还是决定冒一次险，他把香烟放在唇间，划着了火柴，急急忙忙地吸了一口就吹灭了火。几乎是与此同时，一颗子弹射了过来，打在护墙上又弹了回来。狙击手又吸了一口就掐灭了烟，低低地骂了一句就爬到了左边。他小心翼翼地从护墙内探出身来窥望，一道光闪过，一颗子弹嗖的一声贴着他的头皮飞了过去，他立刻缩了回来。他根据看到的闪光判断出子弹是从街道对面射过来的。

他滚到后面的烟囱旁边，在烟囱后面缓缓地立起身来。对面的狙击手隐在夜幕中看不见，却见一辆装甲车驶过小桥，向这条街开来。装甲车停在街对面的五十米处，马达的喷气声声声在耳。狙击手的心跳如捣，越来越快，是敌军的车，他想开枪，可他知道没用，因为子弹绝对无法穿透那个灰色庞然大物的钢制外壳。

接着，从临街街角走过来了一个裹着破破烂烂披肩的老太太，她开始跟装甲车炮塔里的机枪手说着什么，边说边用手指着这个狙击手所在的房顶——肯定是在告密。炮塔开了，露出了机枪手的头和肩，他朝老太太所指的方向瞭望。狙击手立刻端起枪来开了火，机枪手的头重重地落到炮塔的侧壁上。老太太向临街冲去。狙击手又开了一枪，老太太尖叫一声转了个圈，掉进街沟里。

突然，对面的屋顶飞来一颗子弹，狙击手骂了一句，手中的枪咣当一声砸到了屋顶上。狙击手蹲下拾枪，却没有捡起来，他的前臂中弹了。他低声说道："主啊，我中弹了。"

他旋即在屋顶上卧倒，爬回护墙旁。他用手摸了摸受伤的右胳膊。没有痛感，只有麻木的感觉，好像胳膊被砍断了似的。

他迅速从口袋里掏出小刀，抵着护墙把刀打开，用刀把血浸透了的袖子划开。

他拿出战地敷料袋，用刀把袋子挑开，敲碎碘酒瓶颈，把药滴在伤口上，一阵痉挛似的痛感立刻传遍了全身。最后，他把药棉放在伤口上，用战地敷料袋裹住，用牙叼着袋子，把伤口包扎起来。子弹打到了骨头上，骨头一定已经碎了。他贴着护墙静静地躺着，紧闭双眼咬紧牙关忍着痛。

下面的街道一片寂静，装甲车很快从桥上退了下去，机枪手已经死亡，头还在炮塔上耷拉着，老太太的尸体静静地躺在沟里。

这个负了伤的年轻狙击手躺了很久，一面养伤，一面盘算着怎么逃走，因为天一亮，屋顶上的自己就会被发现，被打死，而对面的狙击手是自己逃跑的障碍，所以必须杀掉他，可是自己已经不能用步枪了，只能用手枪来凑合，他终于心生一计。

他把帽子摘下来，放到步枪的枪尖上，然后把步枪慢慢举过护墙，举到街对面能够看到的地方。几乎与此同时出现了反馈，一颗子弹从帽子中间穿过。狙击手把步枪向前倾了倾，让帽子掉到了街上，然后用左手抓住步枪的中间部分，让手从屋顶上无力地耷拉下来。少顷，他松开手，让步枪掉到街上。随后，他扑倒在屋顶上，把手收了回来。

他尽快向左侧爬去，同时窥视着对面的屋顶的一角，发现自己的计策已经奏效：对面的狙击手看到掉落的帽子和步枪，还以为击中了敌人，所以此时正站在一排低矮的烟囱前朝这边张望，那个人头部的轮廓在西方天幕的映衬下清晰可见。

共和党的狙击手微微一笑，提起左轮手枪架在护墙檐上，距离大约有50码，在暗淡的光线下射击不容易，而且右手还疼得厉害，好像有成千上万个魔鬼在捣乱。目标倒是稳定的，可是由于急迫和紧张，他的手在颤抖。他抿了抿嘴，鼻子深深吸了口气，开了枪。

硝烟散尽之后，他向对面窥望，不禁惊喜地叫出了声：他的敌人已经被击中，正在垂死的痛苦中跟跟跄跄地挣扎，他企图在护墙上站稳脚跟，却慢慢地梦幻般地向前栽落了下去，步枪从手中掉落下来，砸在护墙上。接着，屋顶上的垂死的狙击手向前倒了下去，身体在空中翻了几翻，随着沉闷的砰的一声，摔到街上，一动不动了。

看到敌人倒了下去，狙击手耸了耸肩，心中对战争的渴望消失得无影无踪，代之以被懊悔刺痛的心，大颗大颗的汗珠从额头上冒了出来，牙齿也在打战，他开始结结巴巴地自言自语，诅咒这场战争，诅咒自己，诅咒所有的人。他看了看手里还冒着烟的枪，骂了一句就把它扔到了地下，手枪震动着，一颗子弹嗖的一声从他的耳旁飞过，他一惊，恢复了理智，神经也稳定了，恐惧之云被吹散，他哈哈大笑起来。

他从口袋里掏出了那瓶威士忌，一仰脖喝了个精光，在酒精的作用下，他胆子又大了起来。他打算找连长报告情况，于是捡起手枪放进口袋，在晨曦中向下面的房子爬去。爬到临近街口时，他突然按捺不住好奇心，想要看看自己打死的那个狙击手是谁，因为不论对方是谁，他都认为对方也是个出色的狙击手。他想看看是不是认识对方，也许在军队没有分裂以前，他们在同一个连队呢。他决定冒险去看一眼，他环顾四周，发现街的那头战火很猛，而这头却是一片寂静。

他冲过街道，一挺机枪在他周围射出一串冰雹似的子弹，他都躲过去了。他一下子趴倒在那个狙击手的尸体旁，机枪停止了射击。

他把死尸翻了过来，看到的是自己哥哥的脸。

The Snipers

By Liam O'Flaherty

The long June twilight faded into night. Dublin lay enveloped in darkness but for the dim light of the moon that shone through fleecy clouds, casting a pale light as of approaching dawn over the streets and the dark waters of the Liffey. Around the beleaguered Four Courts the heavy guns roared. Here and there through the city, machine guns and rifles broke the silence of the night, spasmodically, like dogs barking on lone farms. Republicans and Free Staters were waging civil war.

On a rooftop near O'Connell Bridge, a Republican sniper lay watching. Beside him lay his rifle and over his shoulders was slung a pair of field glasses. His face was the face of a student, thin and ascetic, but his eyes had the cold gleam of the fanatic. They were deep and thoughtful, the eyes of a man who is used to looking at death.

He was eating a sandwich hungrily. He had eaten nothing since morning. He had been too excited to eat. He finished the sandwich, and, taking a flask of whiskey from his pocket, he took a short drought. Then he returned the flask to his pocket. He paused for a moment, considering whether he should risk a smoke. It was dangerous. The flash might be seen in the darkness, and there were enemies watching. He decided to take the risk. Placing a cigarette between his lips, he struck a match, inhaled the smoke hurriedly and put out the light. Almost immediately, a bullet flattened itself against the parapet of the roof. The sniper took another whiff and put out the cigarette. Then he swore softly and crawled away to the left. Cautiously he raised himself and peered over the parapet. There was a flash and a bullet whizzed over his head. He dropped immediately. He had seen the flash. It came from the opposite side of the street.

He rolled over the roof to a chimney stack in the rear, and slowly drew himself up behind it. His enemy was under cover. Just then an armored car came across the bridge and advanced slowly up the street. It stopped on the opposite side of the street, fifty yards ahead. The sniper could hear the dull panting of the motor. His heart beat faster. It was an enemy car. He wanted to fire, but he knew it was useless. His bullets would never pierce the steel that covered the gray monster.

Then round the corner of a side street came an old woman, her head covered by a tattered shawl. She began to talk to the man in the turret of the car. She was pointing to the roof where the sniper lay—an informer. The turret opened. A man's head and shoulders appeared, looking toward the sniper. The sniper raised his rifle and fired. The head fell heavily on the turret wall. The woman darted toward the side street. The sniper fired again. The woman whirled round and fell with a shriek into the gutter.

Suddenly from the opposite roof a shot rang out and the sniper dropped his rifle with a curse. The rifle clattered to the roof. He stooped to pick the rifle up. He couldn't lift it. His forearm was dead. "Christ," he muttered, "I'm hit."

Dropping flat onto the roof, he crawled back to the parapet. With his left hand he felt the injured right forearm. There was no pain—just a deadened sensation, as if the arm had been cut off.

Quickly he drew his knife from his pocket, opened it on the breast-work of the parapet, and ripped open the sleeve.

Then taking out the field dressing, he ripped open the packet with his knife. He broke the neck of the iodine bottle and let the bitter fluid drip into the wound. A paroxysm of pain swept through him. He placed the cotton wadding over the wound and wrapped the dressing over it. He tied the ends with his teeth. Then he lay against the parapet, and, closing his eyes, he made an effort of will to overcome the pain.

In the street beneath all was still. The armoured car had retired speedily over the bridge, with the machine-gunner's head hanging lifelessly over the turret. The woman's corpse lay still in the gutter.

The sniper lay still for a long time nursing his wounded arm and planning escape. Morning must not find him wounded on the roof. The enemy on the opposite roof covered his escape. He must kill that enemy and he could not use his rifle. He had only a revolver to do it. Then he thought of a plan.

Taking off his cap, he placed it over the muzzle of his rifle. Then he pushed the rifle slowly over the parapet, until the cap was visible from the opposite side of the street. Almost immediately there was a report, and a bullet pierced the centre of the cap. The sniper slanted the rifle forward. The cap slipped down into the street. Then catching the rifle in the middle, the sniper dropped his left hand over the roof and let it hang, lifelessly. After a few moments he let the rifle drop to the street. Then he sank to the roof, dragging his hand with him.

Crawling quickly to the left, he peered up at the corner of the roof. His ruse had succeeded. The other sniper, seeing the cap and rifle fall, thought he had killed his man. He was now standing before a row of chimney, looking across, with his head clearly silhouetted against the western sky.

The Republican sniper smiled and lifted his revolver above the edge of the parapet. The distance was about fifty yards — a hard shot in the dim light, and his right arm was paining him like a thousand devils. He took a steady aim. His hand trembled with eagerness. Pressing his lips together, he took a deep breath through his nostrils and fired.

Then, when the smoke cleared he peered across and uttered a cry of joy. His enemy had been hit. He was reeling over the parapet in his death agony. He struggled to keep his feet, but he was slowly falling forward, as if in a dream. The rifle fell from his grasp, hit the parapet.

Then the dying man on the roof crumpled up and fell forward. The body turned over and over in space and hit the ground with a dull thud. Then it lay still.

The sniper looked at his enemy falling and he shuddered. The lust of battle died in him. He became bitten by remorse. The sweat stood out in beads on his forehead. His teeth chattered, he began to gibber to himself, cursing the war, cursing himself, cursing everybody. He looked at the smoking revolver in his hand, and with an oath he hurled it to the roof at his feet. The revolver went off with the concussion and the bullet whizzed past the sniper's head. He was frightened back to his senses by the shock. His nerves steadied. The cloud of fear scattered from his mind and he laughed.

Taking the whiskey flask from his pocket, he emptied it at a draught. He felt reckless under the influence of the spirit. He decided to look for his company commander, to report. He picked up his revolver and put it in his pocket. Then he crawled down through the skylight to the house underneath. When the sniper reached the laneway on the street, he felt a sudden curiosity as to the identity of the enemy sniper whom he had killed. He decided that he was a good shot, whoever he was. He wondered did he know him. Perhaps he had been in his own company before the split in the army. He decided to risk going over to have a look at him. He peered round. In the upper part of the street there was heavy firing, but around here all was quiet.

The sniper darted across the street. A machine-gun tore up the ground around him with a hail of bullets，but he escaped. He threw himself face downward beside the corpse. The machine-gun stopped.

Then the sniper turned over the dead body and looked into his brother's face.

仇　家

【苏格兰】H.H. 芒罗

　　冬夜，他站在喀尔巴阡山东部山嘴一个莽莽苍苍的丛林间虎视眈眈，凝神倾听，似乎在寻找视力范围内和手中的来福枪射程中的什么猎物——他在等待仇家，黑森林的主人尤里奇·冯·格朗威茨。

　　格朗威茨的森林占地面积大，林中猎物多，令人生羡，那是他的祖父在世时，通过一场诉讼，从杰傲手中夺得的，人们至今还在议论这场蹊跷的官司。如果说格朗威茨在这世上还有一个憎恶诅咒的人的话，那就是杰傲，自孩提时起，两人就大有欲饮对方之血、啖对方之肉的夙愿。今夜，在这个黑暗时分，林子里弥漫着骚动和不安，连小动物们都迟迟不肯入眠。在这样的荒僻之所面对面会见仇家，而周围又没有别人，是他平生的大愿。他从巨大的山毛榉树树身的后面迈步出来，与要找的人撞了个正着。

　　两个仇家死死地盯着对方，一声不吭，两个人的手里都握着枪，胸中涌动着深仇大恨，都欲置对方于死地而后快。就这样过了很长时间，突然一场暴风雨从天而降，一声霹雳在头顶炸响，俩人不及躲闪，被一棵棵山毛榉树压倒了。格朗威茨的一只胳膊压在身下，已经失去了知觉，另一只胳膊和两条腿被缠在树枝里，动弹不得，亏得穿的是厚重的猎靴，脚才没被压碎。很明显，骨折虽然没有看起来那么严重，但如果没人来救的话，他就只能保持这个姿势。树枝划破了他的脸，他眨掉眼睫毛上的血珠，才看到了灾难的全景：杰傲就躺在他的身旁，离他那么近，假如是在平时，他差不多可以够到他，杰傲还活着，还在挣扎，却跟他一样动弹不得。

庆幸自己还活着，但仇人却也幸免于难，于是，尤里奇吐出了一句虔诚的感恩和恶毒的诅咒。杰傲停止了挣扎听了听，迸发出一声短促的狞笑。"你本该丧命，可你毕竟被缠住了，被缠了个结实。哦，真是笑话，尤里奇·冯·格朗威茨在自己巧取豪夺的林子里嚎叫，真是报应！"说完，他又哈哈大笑起来，声音里都是嘲讽残忍的味道。

尤里奇反唇相讥："我陷在自己的林子里，等我的人来救，比你在邻居的土地上因偷窃被抓了个现行却不能脱身的感觉好得多，你个不要脸的。"

杰傲沉默了一会儿，然后安静地答道："我今夜也带了人到林子里，就在我后面不远处，他们会先到来救我，把我身上该死的树枝挪开，不费吹灰之力地把这个大树干砸到你头上。等你的人来的时候，会发现你已经被倒了的山毛榉树砸死了。出于礼节，我会向你的家人吊唁的。"

尤里奇勃然大怒，言辞激烈："这种暗示没用。我想我才不会装模作样地向你的家人正式吊唁呢。"

俩人唇枪舌剑，都想在嘴上占上风，其实心里都清楚自己人要找到自己需要花很长时间，至于谁的人能先到则纯属运气。

俩人都放弃了挣扎，格朗威茨用能腾出的那只手从大衣口袋里抽出了一瓶酒，费了好大劲儿才喝到嘴里。酒对受了伤的人有热身和激活身体的作用，他看了看忍着剧痛一声不吭的敌人，心中升起一丝怜意。

"我把酒扔给你，你能够得着吗？"尤里奇突然开口说道。"咱们一起喝吧，即使今晚你我中间有一个人会死。"

"不，我几乎什么都看不见，眼睛周围都被血糊住了，再说，我什么时候都不跟仇人喝酒。"杰傲回击道。

格朗威茨随即说道："邻居，我改了主意，如果我的人先来，我要他们先救你，就像你是我的客人一样。你我像鬼似的争吵了一辈子，今天夜里我躺在这里渐渐想明白了，我们以前都是傻瓜，生活中有比边界纠纷更美好的事情。邻居，如果你肯捐弃前嫌的话，我……我愿意邀请你做我的朋友。"

杰傲半天没有反应，格朗威茨猜他可能是疼昏过去了。接着，杰傲慢吞吞地说道："如果你我携手开车出现在市场广场，整个地区的舆论一定会为之大哗，活着的人从来没有见过格朗威茨家族的人跟杰傲家族的人友好地说过话。假如我俩今夜捐弃前嫌，林子里的乡亲们从此有了安宁的日子，你可以在我家过夜，我节日也会去你的城堡吃饭……你应该跟我一起去打猎才是。我这辈子除了仇恨你之外，没想过别的，而你在这个弥留时刻，却主动给我酒喝……格朗威茨，我愿意做你的朋友。"

一时间，两人都陷入了沉思，脑海里翻腾着这个戏剧性的让步所带来的奇妙的突变，同时，心中暗暗祈祷自己的人先到，这样，就可以抢先给予昔日的敌人、今日的朋友以礼遇了。

风势稍缓，格朗威茨随即打破了沉默："咱们一起喊救命吧，一起喊声音会传得远些。"他们喊了，却没有回音，格朗威茨说："再喊。"

又沉寂了几分钟，格朗威茨欢叫起来："我看到了一群影子。"

俩人提高嗓门，竭尽全力又喊了起来："他们听到我们的声音了！他们停下了脚步，现在，他们看到我们了，他们正向我们跑来，大约有九个人或者十个人。"格朗威茨告诉杰傲。

"这么说是你的人，我只带了七个人。"杰傲答道。

"他们在全速前进，勇敢的小伙子们。"格朗威茨兴冲冲地说。"是你的人吗？是你的人吗？"杰傲迫不及待地问道，因为格朗威茨没有回答。

"不是。"格朗威茨苦笑了一声，声音中透着恐惧。

"那是谁？"杰傲急忙追问道。

"是狼。"

The Interlopers

By H. H. Munro

In a forest of mixed growth somewhere on the eastern spurs of the Carpathians, a man stood on winter night watching and listening, as though he waited for some beast of the woods to come within the range of his vision, and, of his rifle. But the game for whose presence was Ulrich von Gradwitz, who patrolled the dark forest in quest of a human enemy.

The forest lands of Gradwitz were of wide extent and well stocked with game; was the most jealously guarded of all its owner's territorial possessions. A famous law suit, in the days of his grandfather, had wrested it from the illegal possession of a neighboring family; If there was a man in the world whom he detested and wished ill to it was Georg Znaeym, as boys they had thirsted for one another's blood, and tonight, there was movement and unrest among the creatures that were wont to sleep through the dark hours. If only on this lone spot, he might come across Georg Znaeym, man to man, with none to witness—that was the wish that was uppermost in his thoughts. And as he stepped round the trunk of a huge beech he came face to face with the man he sought.

The two enemies stood glaring at one another for a long silent moment. Each had a rifle in his hand, each had hate in his heart and murder uppermost in his mind. A fierce shriek of the storm had been answered by a splitting crash over their heads, and ere they could leap aside a mass of falling beech tree had thundered down on them. Ulrich von Gradwitz found himself stretched on the ground, one arm numb beneath him and the other held almost as helplessly in a tight tangle of forked branches, while both legs were pinned beneath the fallen mass. His heavy shooting-boots had saved his feet from being crushed to pieces, but if his fractures were not as serious as they might have been, at least it was evident that he could not move from his present position till someone came to release him. The descending twig had slashed the skin of his face, and he had to wink away some drops of blood from his eyelashes before he could take in a general view of the disaster. At his side, so near that under ordinary circumstances he could almost have touched him, lay Georg Znaeym, alive and struggling, but obviously as helplessly pinioned down as himself.

Relief at being alive and exasperation at his captive plight brought a pious thank offerings and sharp curses to Ulrich's lips. Georg stopped his struggling for a moment to listen, and then gave a short, snarling laugh. "So you're not killed, as you ought to be, but you're caught, anyway," he cried; "caught fast. Ho, what a jest, Ulrich von Gradwitz snared in his stolen forest. There's real justice for you!" And he laughed again, mockingly and savagely.

"I'm caught in my own forest-land," retorted Ulrich. "When my men come to release us you will wish, perhaps, that you were in a better plight than caught poaching on a neighbor's land, shame on you."

Georg was silent for a moment; then he answered quietly: "I have men, too, in the forest tonight, close behind me, and they will be here first and do the releasing. When they drag me out from under these damned branches it won't need much clumsiness on their part to roll this mass of trunk right over on the top of you. Your men will find you dead under a fallen beech tree. For form's sake I shall send my condolences to your family."

"It is an unuseful hint," said Ulrich fiercely. "I don't think I can decently send any message of condolence to your family."

Both men spoke with the bitterness of possible defeat before them, for each knew that it might be long before his men would seek him out or find him; it was a bare matter of chance which party would arrive first on the scene.

Both had now given up the useless struggle to free themselves from the mass of wood that held them down; Ulrich limited his endeavors to an effort to bring his one partially free arm near enough to his outer coat pocket to draw out his wine flask. Even when he had accomplished that operation it was long before he could manage to get any of the liquid down his throat. nevertheless, the wine was warming and reviving to the wounded man, and he looked across with something like a throb of pity to where his enemy lay, just keeping the groans of pain and weariness from crossing his lips.

"Could you reach this flask if I threw it over to you？" asked Ulrich suddenly; "Let us drink, even if tonight one of us dies."

"No, I can scarcely see anything; there is so much blood caked round my eyes," said Georg, "and in any case I don't drink wine with an enemy."

"Neighbor," he said presently, "I've changed my mind. If my men are the first to come you shall be the first to be helped, as though you were my guest. We have quarreled like devils all our lives. Lying here tonight thinking I've come to think we've been rather fools; there are better things in life than getting the better of a boundary dispute. Neighbor, if you will help me to bury the old quarrel I— I will ask you to be my friend."

Georg Znaeym was silent for so long that Ulrich thought, perhaps, he had fainted with the pain of his injuries. Then he spoke slowly, "How the whole region would stare and gabble if we rode into the market-square together. No one living can remember seeing a Znaeym and a von Gradwitz talking to one another in friendship. And what peace there would be among the forester folk if we ended our feud tonight. You would come and keep the night beneath my roof, and I would come and feast on some high day at your castle … and you should come and shoot with me I never thought to have wanted to do other than hate you all my life, but I think I have changed my mind about things too, this last half-hour. And you offered me your wine flask…Ulrich von Gradwitz, I will be your friend."

For a space both men were silent, turning over in their minds the wonderful changes that this dramatic reconciliation would bring about. And each prayed a private prayer that his men might be the first to arrive, so that he might be the first to show honorable attention to the enemy that had become a friend.

Presently, as the wind dropped for a moment, Ulrich broke silence. "Let's shout for help, " he said: "our voices may carry a little further if we called together." "Together again, " said Ulrich a few minutes later, after listening in vain for an answering halloo.

Ulrich gave a joyful cry. "I can see figures."

Both men raised their voices in as loud a shout as they could muster. "They hear us! They've stopped. Now they see us. They're running down the hill towards us, about nine or ten, " cried Ulrich.

"Then they are yours, " said Georg, "I had only seven out with me."

"They are making all the speed they can, brave lads, " said Ulrich gladly.

"Are they your men? " asked Georg. "Are they your men? " he repeated impatiently as Ulrich did not answer.

"No ," said Ulrich with a bitter laugh and hideous fear.

"Who are they? " asked Georg quickly.

"Wolves."

交　易

　　拉各南方医学院的标本室一如既往的寒冷潮湿，散发着刺鼻的福尔马林的味道。身材矮小、体重只有六十公斤的莱纳斯·埃特把大约八十公斤重的冷藏尸体标本从巨大的水箱里拖出来摆到铝制桌子上，技艺已经炉火纯青。不到一个小时，已经拉出了十二具，足够本院的学生上解剖课用的了。两小时以后，这位四十岁的助手还要把尸体拖回水箱冷藏。他摘下橡胶手套和围裙，环顾着标本室，迷醉于荧光灯下尸体的美，好像那不是死尸，而是活生生的午睡的人体。

　　墙上的钟敲五点，学生们拖着脚走了进来，"下午好，莱纳斯先生。"学生们齐声向他问好，他也微笑着问候他们。他做实验准备员已有二十年，在学生中很受欢迎。他有时内心妒忌他们锦衣华服和无忧无虑的气质风度，因为他自己的七个孩子缺乏的正是这些东西，但他还是暗自祈祷自己的孩子将来也能在他们中间占有一席之地。

　　莱纳斯走出了标本室，沐浴在午后灿烂的阳光里，却发现自己的大儿子彼特在等他：

　　"爸爸，妈妈让我问你艾尔弗雷德和玛丽是不是跟你在一起？"

　　"跟我在一起？他们怎么会跟我在一起？我不是告诉他俩去山姆大叔干活的地方等你去接吗？"

　　"我……我不知道你这么嘱咐他们的……我……我没去山姆大叔

那里找过。”

“你没去那里找过？”

“没，爸爸，我……我……”

“你可真笨，你来之前应该先核实一下，再跑到这里来。”莱纳斯大声喊道，然后回标本室。他想，这个大傻瓜，竟然舍近求远，不先去山姆的车间看看就大老远地跑到这里。莱纳斯回到岗位之前看了看表，差二十分六点，一想到即将到手的财富，他不禁快乐地战栗了一下，他又笑了。如果这次交易顺利，他就可以提前退休了，尽管他并不是不喜欢现在的工作，相反，他很享受这份工作。这份工作除了工资之外还有这份职业带来的外快。过去，死于交通事故或者自杀的无名尸体并不稀缺，而今，由于交通事故的减少和医学院的剧增，尸体成了抢手货，每具尸体高达三千奈拉。研究胚胎学和先天疾病所必需的童尸更是稀罕物。

因为他有为各南方医学院购买尸体的权利，他从这一生意上赚外快。他购买尸体的技术越来越熟练，他不仅为本院买，而且还自己出钱买进以后转手卖给其他学院、公司，甚至是别的买主。尽管妻子一再劝阻他不要收购来历不明的尸体，他依然满不在乎地通过各种渠道收购尸体。他的经营范围扩大了，很快出现了供不应求的局面。尽管莱纳斯在报纸上也看过婴儿尸体交易不道德行为的报道，莱纳斯依然执迷不悟，继续做他的尸体买卖。他对妻子解释说：“只要我没杀人，我就不用担惊受怕，我的工作只是买进卖出。”

钟敲六点，莱纳斯兴奋起来，他环顾四周，看了看忙碌的师生们，解剖学讲师莫里斯医生此时正绕着桌子解答学生们提出的问题，莱纳斯知道他每次跑出去赴约，都不会有人找他。

六点十五分，詹姆斯在标本室门口探头探脑，向莱纳斯招手，莱纳斯心跳如捣，溜了出来。詹姆斯指着停车场附近一棵芒果树下的三个人说道："他们已经来了。"他们往那三个人所在的地方走的时候，詹姆斯又补充道："就像我跟你说过的那样，这桩生意是正当合法生意，你没什么好怕的。"

他很快跟三人组的头目开始讨价还价起来，这个头目身体健壮，五短身材，左眼瞎了。他对莱纳斯解释说："我们平均每星期能给你提供三具尸体，直到你不再要货为止。"

每星期三具尸体？莱纳斯咂了咂嘴，有了这个量，不久就能满足客户的要求。

"每具尸体一千奈拉，提前付款。"独眼人又补充道。

莱纳斯兴奋得快要发疯了，以一千奈拉这个价格收进，再以五千奈拉卖出的话，每具尸体可净赚四千！十具就赚四万！他满脑袋都是数字，所以独眼人接下来说的话他都没听见，他只脱口而出了一句话：

"我希望送来的货里有一两具童尸。"

"小意思，我的兄弟，"独眼人答道。"事实上，每批货里至少有一具童尸。"

"至少一具？"莱纳斯的气都喘不匀了，发热的脑袋进一步计算着，这会给自己带来六千奈拉的大赚头。

"是的，先生。我们可以拿第一批货的货款了吗？天色已晚。"独眼人说着，伸出了一只手。莱纳斯的手颤抖着掏出了钱包，数出了这笔钱。他把钱递给独眼人时，不放心地看了詹姆斯一眼。

"没问题，"詹姆斯说道。"你可以预付给他们。"

自称贝洛先生的独眼人数完钱以后握着莱纳斯的手说："今晚八点，你会在标本室的门口发现三个袋子，都是你的。"说完，三个人跟詹姆斯一起开着一辆租来的计程车疾驰而去。

莱纳斯返回标本室，把当天的工作做完，心中狂喜。解剖课拖到很晚才下课，等他回到家里的时候已经七点半了，妻子愁眉苦脸地迎了上来，"莱纳斯，我们没找到艾尔弗雷德。"她说着，泪如泉涌。

"你们找不到谁了？"莱纳斯问道。"玛丽呢？"

"她回来了，她说艾尔弗雷德决定不去山姆大叔那儿，去你办公室了，此后我们就没见过他。"

莱纳斯被吓得目瞪口呆："山姆也没看见他？"

"没见过，我都让大儿子去老师家去问了，他有时候不是会在老师家逗留嘛。"

这时，彼特上气不接下气地跑进屋来：

"爸爸！爸爸，艾尔弗雷德的一些同学说，他们一小时以前看到他跟一个男人上了一辆计程车。"

"一个男人？什么男人？"莱纳斯的声音明显发颤。

"他们说是个独眼人。"彼特补充道。

"一个独什么？"莱纳斯大叫。彼特又重复了一遍自己刚说过的话，与此同时，莱纳斯想到了最近这笔交易，不由得汗出如浆。"基督，上帝之子！我完啦。"他边说边找手电筒。

"莱纳斯，怎么回事？这个人是谁？"埃特夫人问道。可她丈夫听也没听，跌跌撞撞地小跑着向医学院的方向冲去。

半个小时以后，他到了标本室，直奔门口那三个鲜血浸透的袋子。他用小刀割开第一个袋子，用手电筒照了照里面，又割开第二个袋子看了看。他开第三个袋子时手在颤抖，他鼓足勇气打开了最后一个袋子。莱纳斯目不转睛地盯着袋中，发出了一声震耳欲聋的尖叫，这尖叫声在几英里以外都能听到——袋中是他七岁儿子的尸体。

The Deal

The mortuary was as usual: cold, damp, and smelled of the eye-stinging fumes of formalin. As Linus Ette were laying out preserved cadavers on the aluminium tables from the huge formalin tanks. A smallish man of about 60 kilograms body weight, Linus had perfected the art of lifting out the approximately 80 kilograms heavy corpses. In less than an hour, Linus was able to set out the twelve cadavers needed for the medical students anatomy demonstration class at the Lagos Southern Medical School. Then after the two-hour class, the forty-year-old attendant would have to return the bodies to the tanks to ensure preservation. As he peeled off the rubber gloves and apron he glanced round the mortuary, was captivated by the beauty of the cadavers under the fluorescent light. It was as if the bodies were actually alive only sleeping away the afternoon.

As the wall clock chimed five o'clock, the medical students started to shuffle into the room. "Good evening, Mr. Ette," the students chorused as Linus smiled and returned their greetings. After more than twenty years at the job, Linus was very popular with the students, though he sometimes envies them their good clothes and carefree attitudes, qualities which his seven children could not afford. But he secretly prayed that some of his children would one day take their place among the students.

Linus went outside into the brightness of the afternoon light, only to meet Peter, his first son, waiting for him.

"Papa, Mama said to ask whether Alfred and Mary are with you？"

"With me? How can they be with me? Didn't I tell them to go and wait at Uncle Sam's place from where you were to get them？"

"I…I don't know that you told them that. I···I haven't checked Uncle Sam's place."

"You didn't check there？"

"No, Papa, I…I…"

"You must be stupid. You should have first checked there before rushing here，" Linus shouted before going back to the mortuary. The silly idiot, he thought. Imagine coming all that way here instead of checking at Sam's workshop which was nearer to the house. As he returned to his post Linus glanced at the clock. It was still twenty minutes to six and a joyous thrill went through him at the thought of what awaited him. Again he smiled. If the deal came through, he might even retire earlier than he had planned, not that he didn't like his present job; in fact, the opposite was the case, he enjoyed it. And apart from his regular pay, there were other moneymaking opportunities that came with the job. In the past, corpses were very much available but now, with the reduced incidence of traffic accidents and an upsurge in the number of new medical schools in the country, corpses had become scare, with pieces as high as three thousand naira per body. Very much in demand were cadavers of embryos, necessary for the study of embryology as well as congenital diseases.

Since Linus had full authority to purchase cadavers for Southern University Medical School, he made additional money from this business. He had become so skillful in buying corpses that he started reselling some of them to other medical schools and firms, as well as other buyers. Despite his wife's admonitions, he continued to purchase the corpses from virtually anywhere. In spite of this warning, Linus expanded his business of buying and selling corpses from any sources. Soon he was swamped with more requests than he could cope with. Although Linus had read in the papers about unscrupulous people who were engaged in a baby-selling business, Linus continued on with his body-selling business. He explained to his wife, "As long as I don't kill anybody, I have nothing to worry about. My work is just to buy and sell."

The clock soon stuck six o'clock and Linus was excited. He glanced round the mortuary, happy to see that the class was still busy with Dr. Morris, the anatomy lecturer who was now going round the tables answering students'questions. Linus knew he wouldn't be missed whenever he decided to dash out for his appointment.

At a quarter past six, James peeped into the mortuary and

beckoned to Linus. His heart now racing madly, Linus quietly sneaked outside to join James at the door. "They are here already," James said, pointing to three men who stood under a mango tree near the car park. "As I told you, this is going to be good, honest deal so you have nothing to be afraid of," James added as they walked to the men.

The discussion quickly got underway with the leader of the three men, a short, stocky man with a bad left eye, explaining things to Linus. "We shall be supplying you an average of three corpses every week until you don't want anymore."

Three corpses a week? Linus smacked his lips. With that kind of supply, he would soon be able to meet the demand of his clients.

"The bodies will be supplied to you at the cost of one thousand naira per body, payable in advance," the man added.

Linus was now wild with excitement. If he bought a body at one thousand naira and sold it at five thousand, he would make a clean profit of four thousand per body! With ten bodies that would come to forty thousand naira! He was so engrossed in his calculations that he didn't even listen again to what the man was saying. All he did was blurt out:

"I hope I can have one or two child corpses in the consignment."

"No sweat, my man," the one-eyed fellow answered. "In fact every consignment will contain at least one child's corpse."

"At least one child?" Linus asked breathlessly as his fevered mind made a further calculation. That will fetch me a cool six thousand.

"Yes, sir. Now can we have the money for the first consignment? It's getting late, " the one-eyed fellow said, thrusting out his hand. Quickly, his hand trembling, Linus brought out his wallet and counted out the money. As he was about to hand the money over to the man, he shot James an anxious look.

"It's all right, " James said. "You can pay them."

After counting the money, the one-eyed fellow who called himself Mr. Bello shook Linus by the hand and said, "By eight o'clock tonight, you will find three sacks by the mortuary door. They are all yours." Then the men entered a hired taxi and drove away with James.

Linus was beside himself with joy as he returned to the mortuary to finish his job for the day. And because the anatomy session dragged on till very late, it wasn't until half-past seven that Linus got home. He was met by his worried-looking wife.

"Linus, we haven't found Alfred, " she said, tears streaking down her face.

"You can't find who? " Linus asked. "How about Marry? "

"She's here. She said that Alfred decided to go to your office instead of to Uncle Sam's place. Since then we haven't seen him."

Linus was aghast: "And Sam didn't see him, too? "

"No, I even asked Peter to check his teacher's house in case he stopped there as he sometimes does."

Just then Peter ran into the house breathlessly.

"Papa! Papa! some of Alfred's classmates said they saw him enter a taxi with a man about an hour ago."

"A man? Which man?" Linus screamed visibly shaken.

"They said the man had a bad eye," Peter added.

"A bad what?" Linus shouted. When Peter repeated himself, Linus'mind went to his recent deal and he broke out in sweat. "Jesus, son of God! I'm finished," he said as he now looked round for a flashlight.

"Linus, what is it? Who is the man?" Mrs. Ette asked but her husband was not listening. He was already half-running, half-stumbling in the direction of the medical school.

He arrived at the mortuary half an hour later and made straight for the three blood-soaked sacks lying by the door. With his penknife, he tore open the first sack, shone his flashlight in side, then went on to the second one. His hands shook as he opened the third sack. He steeled himself opening this last sack. As he stared at the corpse of his seven year old son in the sack, Linus let out an ear-shattering scream that could be heard for miles.

医生为什么迟到

【美】比利·罗斯

一天晚上，快到九点的时候，医生接到了一个电话，"格兰福斯有人找范·艾克医生。"电话里的一个声音说。

"我就是范·艾克。"医生回答。

过了一会儿，范·艾克听到另一个声音说："我是格兰福斯医院的海顿医生。我们医院刚刚收治了一个危重病人，这个男孩头部中弹，现在身体非常虚弱，恐怕不能久保。我们本应该立即进行手术，可你知道，我不是外科医生。"

"我离格兰福斯有六十英里远，"范·艾克医生回答，"你给马萨医生打过电话吗？他住在格兰福斯。"

"他出城了。"海顿医生解释道，"我给你打电话是因为这个男孩从你所在的城市来，他到这里参观，玩枪的时候误伤了自己。"

"你说这个男孩是奥尔班尼人？"范·艾克医生问道，"他叫什么名字？"

"阿瑟·坎宁安。"

"我想我并不认识他，不过我会尽快赶过去。这里在下雪，不过我想我能在十二点以前赶到。"

"我必须事先告诉你这个男孩家里一贫如洗，我认为他们不会给你支付什么报酬。"

"没关系。"范·艾克医生回答。

几分钟以后，医生的车不得不在城郊的一个红灯前停了下来，一个穿黑色旧大衣的男人打开车门，钻了进来。

"接着开，"他说道，"我有枪。"

"我是医生，"范·艾克解释道，"我正赶往医院做手术，患者是一个病危的……"

"少废话，"穿黑色旧大衣的人打断了他的话，"开你的车。"

车出城走了一英里以后，他命令医生停车出去。然后，他开着车沿路而去，丢下医生在纷纷扬扬的雪中怔怔地伫立着。

半个小时以后，范·艾克找到了一部电话，叫了一辆出租车。到了火车站以后，他得知开往格兰福斯的最早的那趟火车要到十二点以后才开。

外科医生范·艾克到达格兰福斯医院时，已是凌晨两点，海顿医生正在等他。

"我已经尽力了，"范·艾克解释道，"可我在路上被劫，我的车也……"

"你能尽力就好，"海顿医生回答，"那个男孩一个小时以前死的。"

两个医生经过医院候诊室的门前，一个穿黑色旧大衣的男人坐在那里，双手抱着头。

"坎宁安先生，"海顿医生对那个人说，"这是范·艾克医生，就是从奥尔班尼一路兼程赶来救你儿子的外科医生。"

Why the Doctor Was Late

By Billy Rose

One Night, a little before nine o'clock, the doctor answered his telephone. "Glens Falls calling Dr. Van Eyck, " said the voice on the telephone.

"This is Dr. Van Eyck speaking, " said the doctor.

A moment later Dr. Van Eyck heard another voice: "This is Dr. Haydon at the hospital in Glens Falls. We have a very sick boy here in our hospital. He has just been brought in with a bullet in his brain. He is very weak and may not live. We should operate at once, but I'm not a surgeon, you know."

"I'm 60 miles from Glens Falls, " said Dr. Van Eyck. "Have you called Dr. Mercer? He lives in Glens Falls."

"He is out of town, " said Dr. Haydon. "I am calling you because the boy comes from your city. He was visiting here and shot himself while playing with a gun."

"You say that the boy is from Albany? " asked Dr. Van Eyck.

"What is his name? "

"Arthur Cunningham."

"I don't think I know him. But I'll get there as soon as I can. It is snowing here, but I think I can get there before 12 o'clock."

"I should tell you that the boy's family is very poor. I don't think they can pay you anything."

"That's all right, " said Dr. Van Eyck.

A few minutes later, the surgeon's car had to stop for a red light at the edge of town. A man in an old black coat opened the door of the car and got in.

"Drive on, " he said. "I've got a gun."

"I'm a doctor, " said Dr. Van Eyck. "I'm on my way to the hospital to operate on a very sick…"

"Don't talk, " said the man in the old black coat. "Just drive."

A mile out of town he ordered the doctor to stop the car and get out. Then the man drove on down the road. The doctor stood there for a moment in the falling snow.

And half hour later Dr. Van Eyck found a telephone and called a taxi. At the railway station he learned that the next train to Glens Falls would not leave until 12 o'clock.

It was after two o'clock in the morning when the surgeon arrived at the hospital in Glens Falls. Dr. Haydon was waiting for him.

"I did my best, " said Van Eyck, "but I was stopped on the road and my car…"

"It was good of you to try，" said Dr. Haydon，"The boy died an hour ago."

The two doctors walked by the door of hospital waiting room. There sat the man in the old black coat，with his head in his hands.

"Mr. Cunningham，" said Dr. Haydon to the man，"this is Dr. Van Eyck. He is a surgeon who came all the way from Albany to try to save your boy."

随意日

　　一号备忘录：公司择定每周的周五为"随意日"，届时员工可以展现异彩纷呈的个性着装风格，本决定立即生效。

　　二号备忘录："随意日"期间，穿弹力紧身衣和超短皮裙，戴"易拉得"领带，系表演性的花边皮带扣，穿软鞋，都属不合适性质。

　　三号备忘录："随意日"指的是衣着服饰上的随意，而非工作态度。各位在星期五选择服装的时候，不要忘记形象是一个人成功的关键因素。

　　四号备忘录：本周五下午四时，在食堂举行"随意日"服饰研讨会，会后有时装表演，要求全体员工参加。

　　五号备忘录：根据本周五举办的研讨会的讨论决定，将组成一个十四人的"随意日"督察队，并为得体的衣着服饰提供相关规范。

　　六号备忘录："随意日"督察队制定了一本三十页的守则，题为《服装随意　公司的标准不随意》，现将其副本转发给全体员工。每周五上班之前，请回忆《你穿什么衣服就是什么样的人》一章，同时参阅清单上的"家常式随意"与"工作式随意"所列款项，来决定当天的衣着服饰。如果你对于某件服饰是否合适心存疑问的话，请于每周五早七点以前致电"随意日"督察队进行咨询。

　　七号备忘录：由于缺乏员工参与，"随意日"取消，从即日起立即生效。

Dressed Down

Memo No.1：to employees：Effective immediately, the company is adopting Friday as Casual Day so that employees may express their diversity.

Memo No.2：Spandex and leather micro-miniskirts are not appropriate attire for Casual Day. Neither are string ties, rodeo belt buckles or moccasins.

Memo No.3：Casual Day refers to dress only, not attitude. When planning Friday's wardrobe, remember image is a key to our success.

Memo No.4：A seminar on how to dress for Casual Day will be held at 4 p.m. Friday in the cafeteria. Fashion Show to follow. Attendance is mandatory.

Memo No.5：As an outgrowth of Friday's seminar, a 14-member Casual Day Task Force has been appointed to prepare guidelines for proper dress.

Memo No.6：The Casual Day Task Force has completed a 30-page manual. A copy of "Relaxing Company Standards" has been mailed to each employee. Please review the chapter "You Are What You Wear", and consult the "home casual" versus "business casual" checklist before leaving for work each Friday. If you have doubts about the appropriateness of an item of clothing, contact your CDTF representative before 7 a.m. on Friday.

Memo No.7: Because of lack of participation, Casual Day has been discontinued, effective immediately.

生活是不是说不好

人在潸然泪下时，学会了哈哈大笑，

人在最悲惨的日子里，学会了人性美好……

人在无感的时候，学会了去感受，

人在没有占有许多的时候，学会了施与。

人在寒冷的时候，学会了取暖……

人在真正卑微地生活时，学会了无畏勇敢。

人在痛不欲生时，学会了生存……

人在只能痛哭流涕时，学会了开怀大笑。

人在低层人身上，学到了高尚的模样……

人在被怀恨在心时，学会了如何去爱别人。

人在颠沛流离时，学会了怎样休养生息，

人在身处绝境时，学到了最高的真义。

人在迷失茫然的时候，了解了自己。

人在身无分文的时候，学会了致富之道……

上述问题似乎个个这么严肃，可是……

生活是不是说不好！？

Isn't Life Funny

I learned to laugh inside my tear,

I learned to be human in my most wretched years...

I learned to feel when I wasn't being touched,

I learned to give when I didn't have much.

I learned to be warm when I was cold...

Living real humbly, I learned to be bold.

I learned to live when I thought it better to die...

I learned to laugh when all I could do was cry.

I learned from below what it's like up above...

While I was hated, I learned how to love.

It was on the move that I learned how to rest,

While at my worst, I learned my best.

It is when I was lost that I learned that I am.

I learned to be rich when I had no money...

These things seem so serious, but hey...

Isn't life funny!?

我终于恍然大悟

我终于恍然大悟……世界上最精彩的课堂是长者的膝前。

我终于恍然大悟……人在热恋，一目了然。

我终于恍然大悟……听到有人对我说："你让我快乐！"这让我快乐。

我终于恍然大悟……世界上最祥和的感觉是娇儿怀中眠。

我终于恍然大悟……仁慈比正确更重要。

我终于恍然大悟……孩子的礼物永远都不该拒绝。

我终于恍然大悟……我在某些方面不能给人援手的时候，我总可以为人祈愿。

我终于恍然大悟……不管生活需要你多么一本正经，每个人都需要一个朋友一起犯二疯癫。

我终于恍然大悟……有时候，人需要一只可以握住的手和一颗善解的心。

我终于恍然大悟……当我还是小孩时，夏夜陪我父亲在几个街区散步，造就了我长大成人后的奇迹。

我终于恍然大悟……生命像一卷卫生纸，越到最后，消耗得越快。

我终于恍然大悟……我们想要什么，上帝并没有就赐给我们什么，我们应该为此而欢喜。

我终于恍然大悟……金钱买不到品位。

我终于恍然大悟……正是那些日常生活的点点滴滴让生命如此壮观。

我终于恍然大悟……在那些人的坚硬外壳下，都隐藏着对欣赏和爱的渴念。

我终于恍然大悟……上帝都没有在一天之内完成一切，何况我呢？

我终于恍然大悟……对事实视而不见，事实不会改变。

我终于恍然大悟……你若蓄谋报复别人，只会让别人继续伤害你。

我终于恍然大悟……可以疗愈一切伤痛的是爱，不是时间。

我终于恍然大悟……我成长的捷径是置身于更聪慧的人中间。

我终于恍然大悟……遇到的每个人都该得到你浅笑问安。

我终于恍然大悟……与爱子同眠，感受他们的鼻息拂面，是人间的至美甘甜。

我终于恍然大悟……世上无完人，直到你有了心上人。

我终于恍然大悟……生命维艰，我更坚韧。

我终于恍然大悟……机会从不走空，你错过的，必有人把握。

我终于恍然大悟……当你受苦受难，幸福也即将靠岸。

我终于恍然大悟……我多希望在父亲去世之前，再告诉他一次我爱他。

我终于恍然大悟……今天应该温柔爱怜地遵守诺言，因为明天就可能食言。

我终于恍然大悟……微笑整容法最物美价廉。

我终于恍然大悟……我不能选择我的感受，但是我可以选择我的做法。

　　我终于恍然大悟……当刚降生的孙儿的小拳握住你的小拇指时，你对生命如此痴恋。

　　我终于恍然大悟……人人都想身居高山之巅，但所有的快乐和成长都出现在攀登的过程中间。

　　我终于恍然大悟……最好只在下列两个场合给人意见：别人问计，生命遇险。

　　我终于恍然大悟……给我的时间越短，我完成的工作未减反添。

I've Learned

I've learned…That the best classroom in the world is at the feet of an elderly person.

I've learned…That when you're in love, it shows.

I've learned…That just one person saying to me, "You've made my day!" makes my day.

I've learned…That having a child fall asleep in your arms is one of the most peaceful feelings in the world.

I've learned…That being kind is more important than being right.

I've learned…That you should never say no to a gift from a child.

I've learned…That I can always pray for someone when I don't have the strength to help him in some other way.

I've learned…That no matter how serious your life requires you to be, everyone needs a friend to act goofy with.

I've learned…That sometimes all a person needs is a hand to hold and a heart to understand.

I've learned…That simple walks with my father around the block on summer nights when I was a child did wonders for me as an adult.

I've learned…That life is like a roll of toilet paper. The closer it gets to the end, the faster it goes.

I've learned…That we should be glad God doesn't give us everything we ask for.

I've learned…That money doesn't buy class.

I've learned…That it's those small daily happenings that make life so spectacular.

I've learned…That under everyone's hard shell is someone who wants to be appreciated and loved.

I've learned…That the Lord didn't do it all in one day. What makes me think I can?

I've learned…That to ignore the facts does not change the facts.

I've learned…That when you plan to get even with someone, you are only letting that person continue to hurt you.

I've learned…That love, not time, heals all wounds.

I've learned…that the easiest way for me to grow as a person is to surround myself with people smarter than I am.

I've learned…That everyone you meet deserves to be greeted with a smile.

I've learned…That there's nothing sweeter than sleeping with your babies and feeling their breath on your cheeks.

I've learned…That no one is perfect until you fall in love with them.

I've learned…That life is tough, but I'm tougher.

I've learned…Those opportunities are never lost; someone will take the ones you miss.

I've learned…That when you harbor bitterness, happiness will dock elsewhere.

I've learned…That I wish I could have told my Dad that I love him one more time before he passed away.

I've learned…That one should keep his words both soft and tender, because tomorrow he may have to eat them.

I've learned…That smile is an inexpensive way to improve your looks.

I've learned…That I can't choose how I feel, but I can choose what I do about it.

I've learned…That when your newly born grandchild holds your little finger in his little fist, that you're hooked for life.

I've learned…That everyone wants to live on top of the mountain, but all the happiness and growth occurs while you're climbing it.

I've learned…That it is best to give advice in only two circumstances: when it is requested and when it is a life threatening situation.

I've learned…That the less time I have to work with, the more things I get done.

图书在版编目（CIP）数据

愿你出走半生　归来仍是少年：英汉对照/（美）朱迪·赛佛斯等著；张白桦译.—北京：中国国际广播出版社，2017.1（2019.1重印）

（译趣坊. 世界微型小说精选）

ISBN 978-7-5078-3784-1

Ⅰ.①愿… Ⅱ.①朱…②张… Ⅲ.①小小说－小说集－世界－英、汉 Ⅳ.①I14

中国版本图书馆CIP数据核字（2016）第299893号

愿你出走半生　归来仍是少年（中英双语）

著　　者	〔美〕朱迪·赛佛斯 等	
译　　者	张白桦	
责任编辑	笑学婧　张娟平	
版式设计	国广设计室	
责任校对	徐秀芮	

出版发行	中国国际广播出版社〔010-83139469　010-83139489（传真）〕
社　　址	北京市西城区天宁寺前街2号北院A座一层
	邮编：100055
网　　址	www.chirp.com.cn
经　　销	新华书店
印　　刷	环球东方（北京）印务有限公司

开　　本	880×1230　1/32
字　　数	200千字
印　　张	8
版　　次	2017 年 1 月　北京第一版
印　　次	2019 年 1 月　第三次印刷
定　　价	26.00元

CRI

欢迎关注本社新浪官方微博

中国国际广播出版社

官方网站 www.chirp.cn